The Human

From **Lift** to **The Road**

Marc Isaacs on his Films

© Marc Isaacs 2018

Text edited by Robert Lambolle

Assisted by Maya Hornick

ISBN 978-1-5272-2777-4

First published by Second Run Limited 2018
www.secondrundvd.com

Design and layout by Robert Riley, RCR Graphics
www.rcrgraphics.co.uk

With thanks to:

Aisling Ahmed
Chris Barwick
Sally Bayly
Nick Bradshaw
Georgina Cammalleri
David Charap
Ben Coulson
Russell Crockett
Rebecca Day
Matej Dimlic
Sergei Dimlic
Michel Duvoisin
Jason Evans
Ben Ferguson
Heidi Fleisher
Rebecca Frankel
Nick Fraser
Max Gogarty
Andrew Hinton
Graeme Hobbs
Lance Hogan
Marianne Hougen-Moraga
Ollie Huddleston
Burt Hunger
Juliett Joffe
David Katznelson

Lucy Kaye
Guy King
Richard Klein
Jo Lapping
Jez Lewis
Becky Lomax
Noel Megahey
Nick Mirsky
Mehelli Modi
Joshua Neal
Paula Nightingale
Jess O'Keefe
Aldo Paternostro
Clare Patterson
Laura Rascarolli
Stephan Riguet
Robert Riley
Shanida Scotland
Michael Stewart
Kate Taunton
Kate Townsend
Emma Tutty
Nadia Von Christierson
Estephan Wagner
Rachel Wexler
Oliver Wright

Table of Contents

All White in Barking (2008)

Foreword By Nick Fraser

When Marc Isaacs makes a film it's more than a story or a set of ideas. He doesn't just show us a person who lives in Barking or Calais or the City or somewhere no-one really quite knows about in North London. We see more than the desk, the worn sofa and the scrubby garden nearby. Isaacs sees past these people in oddly-worn, misshapen clothes and takes his audience to the core of his subjects' lives. People in his films are often isolated and fallible. They speak phrases that may not be eloquent but are always truthful. Are they unhappy or happy? It's hard to be sure. Characters like these can sometimes be found in novels but rarely in films. As a filmmaker, it's clear that Isaacs likes his characters, and we grow to like them too. Their appeal comes from their fallibility, the freedom with which they talk to Isaacs. Always keen to be filmed and to watch footage of themselves. Marc Isaacs' films are not at all depressing. He isn't polemical or factual. He doesn't describe the whole world or filter the environment or tell us too much. But from the smallest scene in an Isaacs film we can understand so much. He gives us a glimpse of an entirely different world and then we walk away. It's difficult to create a great documentary. Alas, television executives are more interested in clichés or fake drama. But Marc Isaacs just watches, day by day. He observes life carefully. Those who appear in his films are not heroes or villains. But they understand their lives, and he shows this, scene by scene. Love, or even understanding, are special gifts. Marc's films are very funny, circuitous and special.

Nick Fraser is the former Commissioning Editor of BBC *Storyville*. He is currently the Editor of the documentary streaming platform, Docsville.

Chapter One

One Man – One Camera

Outside the Court (2011)

Digital imagery is replacing the written word, and subject matter that would have previously been written is now filmed. Brands want video content, everyone films on their phones - even my mum has become a 'filmmaker'. I was lucky enough to have entered filmmaking at the time of Sony's release of the VX1000 camera, the first to use the DV format. Some filmmakers had previously shot on 8mm tape but the VX1000 revolutionised digital documentary film production and allowed for low-cost desktop editing. Whilst the digital revolution has clearly democratised filmmaking by placing the means of production in the hands of the many, the digital camera does not come packaged with a set of eyes that aid the creation of works of art. In fact, to use a drone you don't need eyes at all. In my teaching I have noticed a growing fascination amongst film students with digital cameras and the technological paraphernalia of film production. It's as if the multiple choices available on the market have sent them into a spin. There is now such a strong emphasis on the look of a film that subject matter and substance can often feel like a secondary concern.

I have always shot my own films and whilst I tend to work with one or two researchers during the filming period and have always worked with a film editor, the production of sound and image has fallen upon my shoulders. Those small-scale cameras have changed a little over the years and holding them has become a part of my life. It is the act of holding the camera that has shaped my approach to filmmaking. When the camera zooms in, it is my zoom. When it pans, it is my pan. The small digital camera has enabled a particular style of filming that I've deployed since my first film.

It has allowed for a very direct relationship with the characters in my work, and my films often shatter the fourth wall, largely due to the informal nature of the technology. Working simultaneously as cameraman, soundman and director has facilitated the development of a strong subjectivity - my shadow hangs heavily over all my films. I encourage people to address me directly and to interact with the camera, and my voice from behind it is a strong feature of my work. When I started out I was aware of the notion of the 'fly on the wall' but found myself naturally dismissing this approach. In *Lift* (2001) the fly on the wall expires at the end of the film. I realised quickly that pure observation wasn't for me but, nevertheless, observing people is a strong part of my character. Between the ages of seven and fifteen I spent much of my time standing between football goal posts on various muddy fields in suburbia. Nervously watching the drama unfolding in front of me, I would suddenly be forced into action, cast as hero or villain. This is the way the goalkeeper functions and it has parallels with that of the filmmaker. It forced me into the role of the observer early on and enhanced the 'outsider' feeling that, by the age of seven, was already a pronounced feature of my personality.

In my films, I have taken on the role of the provocateur by setting up scenes, intervening and re-arranging - the fly in *Lift*, for instance, was purchased from a local pet-shop. The informal and independent nature of the process appeals to my character and from the outset I have deployed the conjuror's 'smoke and mirrors'. Despite this, my instinct leans towards acknowledging my own presence and revealing the filmmaking process itself.

Some filmmakers have fixed or predetermined ideas and know exactly what they want to say in a film before embarking on its making. That is not the case with me. I often don't know exactly what I am searching for until I find it. The relatively compact and cheap technology involved has allowed for long production periods that can incorporate false turns, surprising tangents and new discoveries. My films make me, as much as I make them. I work in a state of constant flux and am always ready to change direction. Each film is a result of a long conversation with reality. I embrace doubt but I know what I like and how I feel. I rely on my instinct more than my intellect. I get depressed when reality fails to inspire me but out of this depression fresh ideas emerge. At the beginning of every film project it feels as if there's a mountain to climb but I am confident I will reach the summit eventually. The hairs on the back of my neck occasionally stand up during the filmmaking process. But most of the time I am chasing ghosts and it is when things are not working out that I learn the most about filmmaking. With my lightweight camera in hand, I seek out precious moments and thrive on unpredictability. I borrow ideas from other artists and then make them my own. I am never fully satisfied with my films and I tend to avoid watching them once they are finished.

I didn't watch many art-house features or documentaries until I was in my early twenties. Nor was there a precise moment when I decided to take up filmmaking. But in my final year of university, at the age of 28, I started to write a fiction film-script with a friend. It was a character study set in the world of football hooligans in London in the early 1980s. A few years earlier I had seen a two-part documentary on Channel 4 entitled *The Knockers' Tale* and *Whatever Happened to the Knockers?* – the latter being a ten-year follow-up to the original. It observed the lives of a group of young lads who sold cheap domestic goods by knocking on doors in suburbia. They were all otherwise unemployed and, in some cases, unemployable, and they were also football hooligans. I knew one or two of the people in the film and on first viewing it was as if aspects of my own life were being reflected back to me. It came as a powerful moment of realisation that it was possible to make films about things close to my own experience.

The Knockers' Tale
(Jeff Perks, 1983)

11

My script-writing endeavour fizzled out, however, and instead I found work in a post-production house in London's Soho, followed soon after by a stint as a 'runner' in a production company. Around the same time I bought a domestic camcorder and started filming my home life for practice.

I spent just a few months as a runner before becoming an Assistant Producer on a few documentary films. I began honing my filming skills by shooting characters during the casting process of these works. For five years I closely observed the different directors I was working with. I am especially indebted to Pawel Pawlikowski, with whom I worked on two films over a two-year period, *Twockers* (1998) and *Last Resort* (2000). Working alongside Pawel was my film school. I learned how to think outside of the narrow confines of television documentary conventions and felt inspired to discover my own voice.

Chapter Two

Moments in Time

Before I made *Lift* in 2001 I had never created my own work. I remember being propelled by the excitement of the prospect and can see now how my naivety set me free. For this film I returned to a familiar location. The tower block where the film was set is a stone's throw away from Petticoat Lane market in London's East End, where I worked for a couple of years in my early teens to earn some pocket money. As soon as I met Lilly, the elderly Jewish woman and subsequent 'main' character of the film, I knew that I'd found what I was looking for. Her madcap humour and blunt means of expression were utterly familiar to me. The world she inhabited, alongside Bangladeshis, Jews, Irish, Scots, Poles and West Indians, was a part of London that I felt instinctively at home in.

I never realised at the time, but can see clearly now, that I was discovering the importance of film form and self-imposed limitations. Through the act of filming brief moments of time solely inside a lift - moments in which people are neither at home nor quite out in the world - I had subconsciously created a transient space of reflection. It was as if life had been momentarily paused so that some of the basic questions of existence could be explored. The transient and reflective quality of the film, together with the self-imposed restriction of filming exclusively inside a lift, struck a chord with audiences and I later developed it further by filming on trains, in lorries and on a Roman road, amongst other places.

Transience appeals because it mirrors the impermanence of our condition. Like all of us, I am acutely aware of the fleeting nature of existence and, without over-thinking this, I have found myself again and again creating scenes and, indeed, whole films that express this ephemerality through both form and approach to mise-en-scène. For the 24 minutes and 27 seconds of *Lift* we drift into a metal container and thereby into the lives of its inhabitants; and then, just as effortlessly, we drift out again. We experience the briefest moments of emotional intimacy with the film's characters, yet something of them remains with us after the film ends.

Similarly, in *Calais: The Last Border* (2003), despite spending less than fifteen minutes of screen time with Ijaz from Kabul, one of the film's main protagonists, he is likely to remain in our minds beyond the film's conclusion.

Ijaz from *Calais: The Last Border* (2003)

The experience of the immigrant is also one of transience, which goes some way to explaining why this subject recurs throughout my work. Immigrants often find themselves both physically and psychologically caught in a state of 'inbetweenness'. It can be on a journey from one place to another, as in *Calais: The Last Border*, or dealing with feelings of loss of home on arrival in a new country, as in *The Road – A Story of Life and Death* (2013).

There is a clear link in my mind between transience and the act of distillation that occurs in my filmmaking process. On first consideration, it might appear that there is a contradiction between the idea of transience and the lasting emotional effect of a work, in the sense that transience implies ephemerality. But I have always found the opposite to be true. Just as a still photograph can make a lasting impression, the same can be said of filmed moments in time.

Many of the most emotionally charged scenes in my films are characterised by a sense of brevity. Filmmaking is a process of distillation. It starts with the hatching of an idea and ends on the last day of editing. It is about filming the essence of things and not getting sidetracked by depicting events that lack cinematic or emotional power. It means freeing oneself from notions of objectivity and factual truth. Just because something exists or occurs doesn't mean it should be filmed. In every film and with every character I am presented with numerous filming opportunities, but unless I am convinced of the poetic and emotional potential of a situation I prefer not to pick up the camera. I learned through the making of *Lift* that there are crucial decisions to be made about what to show in a film and what to leave to the imagination of the viewer. In fact, in the early days of shooting the film, before I had made the decision that it would be set entirely in the lift, I tried filming Lilly in her apartment, only to discover that I was making a terrible mistake. The scene was lifeless and I could feel that it revealed far too much of her way of life. Limiting myself solely to the lift provided tension and humour and, of course, it was also an act of provocation. But more importantly, I understood that this decision to conceal would provide a space for the viewer to enter into the work. *Lift* was the precursor of an approach to filmmaking whereby the 'action' is usually more internal than external. In *Outside the Court* (2011), this takes on a physical aspect because we are with the protagonists, not where we would normally be expected to observe the drama unfold - during the hearings inside the court itself - but in those exterior in-between spaces where they await the fateful decision of the judge.

Outside the Court (2011)

When Ijaz, in *Calais: The Last Border*, is at his lowest point, the scene unfolds in the stillness of the port where boats are marooned in the mudflats. We never see him trying to jump on trains or lorries to reach his destination. In the same film, when Tulia describes her suicidal feelings, she is simply seated on her sofa beside her husband reflecting on her troubles. In these scenes nothing is happening... yet everything is happening. There is little physical external movement - the movement is purely internal.

The occurrence of the most delicate and subtle moments of action is often enough for me to build a scene. In the opening scene of *All White in Barking* (2008), Susan is sitting in her conservatory watching her Albanian neighbour through the window. After waving to him, she delivers a monologue that reveals her anxieties and fears of the 'other' in her vicinity. The small detail of the neighbour's presence in the back of the frame brings the scene to life. I had previously tried to film a similar scene, with Susan standing on her doorstep, but it fell flat precisely because of the lack of something she could react to.

When I wanted to construct a scene with Norman, from *Men of the City* (2009), about his decision not to have children. I waited for many months for the right moment before shooting it at night with him in his back garden, knowing that if I created the right atmosphere his reaction to my question would resonate. The 'action' is located on Norman's face as he contemplates his decision. Nothing more is needed to engage the viewer.

Norman from *Men of the City* (2009)

In *Men of the City* there is a very sharp contrast between those characters who are in the flow and movement (or action) of life, like David, the hedge fund manager, and those who are either still (Fakhrul, the signboard holder) or reflective (Steve, the street sweeper who, like the filmmaker, is also an observer of life). In fact, trying to create a reflective space for scenes involving David was so difficult that it became one of the tension points in the film, in which his resistance to my probing is often palpable.

In my view, far too many documentary films are obsessed with 'action' and what we might call 'high drama'. These films get carried away with their own 'dramatic' narrative construction, leaving little or no space for any form of reflection or self-discovery by the viewer. They tend to mimic the narrative linear structure of mainstream fiction films and are often overly sensational.

The filmmaker, Peter Watkins, has described this type of approach very well in his essay 'The Media Crisis', which is about what he terms the mono-form. I am rarely able to engage in these films and often find them exploitative and patronising, both to audiences and the films' contributors. They certainly don't live long in my memory.

I want my audience to find a space for themselves in my films, to be able to reflect on their own lives. I want people to be able to return to them again and again, as I return to the work of those filmmakers who have inspired me over the years. When teaching film students, I often show the same relatively few extracts repeatedly. There is a scene with a woman called Miriam in an Amos Gitai documentary entitled *Wadi 1981-1991*. I must have viewed the scene fifty times, and yet I always watch it with the same intense involvement. It never loses its emotional power because Miriam talks about her struggles in such a beautiful way that something that might be experienced as depressing becomes totally life-affirming. I never tire of this kind of authenticity. Again, nothing very much happens... but everything happens.

Miriam from *Wadi 1981-1991*
(Amos Gitai)

Calais: The Last Border (2003)

Chapter Three

Thoughts on Character

The themes and characters that concern me connect deeply with the emotions and feelings that exist within me. Whilst I rarely turn the camera lens towards myself, my films can in some vital sense be viewed as self-portraits. My characters are often outsiders. I have filmed immigrants, criminals, addicts, racists, the lonely and the delusional, but they are all, ultimately, ordinary everyday people. It might be their 'otherness' that first attracts me to them but I end up finding aspects of myself in all of them. Since they are often conflicted there is a tension at the heart of their existence. These tensions may be emblematic of the times in which we live but they are also existential and borderless. I seek out universal aspects of the human condition because I believe in their existence. If a film's subject isn't broad enough to allow for an emotional exploration of character I am not interested in making it. I seek out psychological insights into character rather than linear plot development. Consequently, I have never made a film in which the subject or central issue overrides this or in which the themes have felt limited from the outset, despite having been offered numerous projects of this nature over the years.

Before I begin thinking seriously about casting, I identify the broad themes of the film and the potential setting. But whatever the specifics of the film, there is a type of character I am attracted to. To find appropriate characters is often extremely time-consuming and takes an enormous amount of persistence; but quite often the encounters seem fated and at that juncture the characters seem to need me as much as I need them. During the making of *Calais: The Last Border* I hit a point in the production when I was desperately searching for an additional character that could bring a sense of history to the film. I remember dreaming up the ideal character and she turned out to be remarkably similar to Tulia, one of the film's main protagonists, whom I discovered a short time afterwards. There needs to be a deep connection between us for the relationship to work. I need to be able to imagine myself in their shoes to fully understand them. They might represent my worst fears or greatest hopes but unless that connection is there I can't consider them for the film.

To make character-based films you need to be able to take a step back, to observe people from a suitable distance. You have to learn to view the familiar in unfamiliar ways and to ask the questions others take for granted. From as far back as I can remember I have carried with me feelings of separateness. I put this partly down to my Jewish upbringing. I did live amongst other Jews in the suburban town where I grew up but most of the inhabitants were white English East Enders who, like my own family, had moved out in search of a more comfortable life. The feeling of separation or difference would be encountered in a neighbour's kitchen through the smell of fried bacon and pork that permeated the atmosphere, or on 'the walk of shame' to the local synagogue on Yom Kippur when, all suited up, we were subjected to the taunts of the non-Jewish kids as we passed by the school gates. I'm sure these experiences have benefited me in my approach to filmmaking.

My characters are authentic and say exactly what they think without self-censoring and they often have a sense of humour. In the casting process I pay attention to their patterns of speech, gestures and self-expressions, much as a writer of fiction would. They need to have a face that tells a thousand stories. After all, it's the face that initially draws us in. I have an enormous responsibility to the people I film not to betray their trust and openness, yet their portrayal in the films is without question purely subjective. I start from the understanding that it's my personal take on their story. I focus on the aspects of their lives that obsess me and cross my fingers that they will ultimately recognise themselves in my portrayal. Like all of us, they live multifaceted lives but what we see in the films is a highly distilled version of their existence. Far more of their real life is concealed, compared to what the film makes visible.

I often play with what I imagine to be the preconceptions of the audience. For example, if we look at the first scene with Michel, the Frenchman in *Outside the Court*, he first appears as a knife-wielding 'madman'. But quite soon, as he reveals his painful childhood, we begin to see a very different character emerge. Similarly, when Tulia (*Calais: The Last Border*) enters the Zoo Bar - and the film - for the first time, we are taken aback by her presence. I have been at many screenings where laughter in the audience has been audible at this moment, only to observe a distinctly different reaction when, later in the film, we hear about her life as a child refugee in an internment camp in Franco's Spain. When Monty is introduced in *All White in Barking*, we have little idea how his experience as a holocaust survivor will eventually impact on the film. It is these personal 'discoveries' that make the experience of the narrative interesting and help elicit feelings of empathy from the audience.

I don't search out extremes and I am keen to avoid sensationalism. Even in *Philip and His Seven Wives* (2006), a film in which it would have been easy to fall into that trap, I adopted a downbeat tone in order to avoid this. Indeed, when I was first introduced to Philip's family I was very unsure about whether to even make the film. It wasn't until I discovered that they were everyday, familiar people that I felt comfortable enough to go ahead with the filming.

Despite focussing on the lives of ordinary people it certainly isn't the case that everybody is suitable for inclusion in a film; and for every one of the people I do end up filming there are always others who, for various reasons, fall out of the running during the research process. Each character must provide emotional development to ensure the narrative momentum of the film. I don't know, and don't have to know at the outset, where I might go with a character. But I do need to be sure of their potential for personal revelation and emotional insight. Often, I invent scenes and provoke reactions to get at my obsessions. If I go too far it becomes clear very quickly and I am forced to rethink my approach. Similarly, if I do not intervene, a promising scene can easily fall flat on its face. Although the characters aren't actors in the conventional sense, there is certainly a dimension of performance that occurs during the process of filming. Sometimes this is self-determined, for instance when the camera follows Tulia (*Calais: The Last Border*) into the opticians where her client is having eye surgery and she is keen to communicate to the camera that her business is thriving. It was a scene I shot early on, when we were still getting to know each other and she viewed her participation in the film as a means of self-promotion. In the following scene, as she waits with her husband for her client's consultation to conclude, I provoke her to reveal her hardships. And now, as if the previous scene was just an 'on-stage' moment, we are privy to what she really feels about her life. Sometimes it is this type of self-presentation that needs to be managed, i.e. directed. So in order to ensure the success of a scene, I will often give the characters specific instructions. When Fakhrul (*Men of the City*) was packing away his chair and signboard to take a tea break, I asked him to speed up the process to intensify a scene that would otherwise have certainly failed.

In the process of constructing character and story, the degree of provocation, direction and intervention varies. Occasionally it can be quite large-scale. The opening scene of *The Road – A Story of Life and Death* is fictitious in the sense that Keelta's journey by ferry and road from Ireland to London was an invention on my part. I had already met and filmed her in London before deciding during the editing of the film to shoot this additional sequence. In fact, it is not even an invention that is faithful to the reality of the journey she previously undertook. She actually arrived in London on a Ryanair flight some months previously. My concern was to communicate the emotion of the experience of leaving home and so I was solely focussed on creating a sequence that would convey those feelings to the audience. Structurally, the film demanded such an opening as an introduction to the setting of the road and Keelta's character. When I test the reaction of people to this scene in my workshops, very few question its authenticity. I remember receiving a nervous phone call from a BBC executive on discovering that this travel sequence was an invention, insisting that the scene be cut so as not to mislead the audience.

Keelta from *The Road – A Story of Life and Death* (2013)

I argued my case that it was of little or no importance if Keelta's journey happened that way or not because the only matter of concern was the emotional truth of the scene. But my plea fell on deaf ears and so the TV version includes a shortened (less 'misleading') version of the scene. There are misleading representations and justified ones, and each filmmaker will decide for themselves where they fall on the spectrum of authenticity. Some of my own interventions are clearly 'labelled', drawing attention to themselves as part of the narrative construction, as is the case with the dinner party scene in *All White in Barking*. This scene was born out of the challenge of developing Susan's character and understanding her apparent fear of the 'other'. I needed to find a way to externalise her prejudice and fear because it was something that was locked in her mind. The idea for the scene was directly related to the research process. I had accidentally encountered Dixon, her Nigerian neighbour, by provoking his ire whilst filming in the street outside his house. Through this, we got talking and, because of the lack of contact between the different ethnicities in the town, the idea occurred to me to bring them together. I knew Susan would be charming in such a scene and that it would therefore turn out to be both comical and touching. Having invested so much time in working on the scene, I had to ensure its success. So I asked Dixon and his wife to cook traditional Nigerian food. Indeed, food became a central metaphor in the film, the motif through which difference and prejudice were played out. Again, I have no issue with intervening in this way because I don't have set ideas regarding what constitutes a documentary film.

Naturally, I form a very close relationship with most of the people I film and they live on in my mind through every festival screening and DVD release. But I only keep in close contact with a small number of them; and, of course, some have passed away. It's a strange feeling to watch a person on the screen who is no longer alive, fixed in that particular filmed moment. For many years, I only once had to deal with the passing of a character during the filming period, though recently it happened twice more, in the same film, *The Road – A Story of Life and Death*. When both Billy and Peggy died it became very difficult for me as I was thrust into a state of sadness at their passing and confusion about how to integrate their deaths into the narrative of the film. With Billy, I was always aware of the seriousness of his condition, especially when I managed to film him in his home. This scene almost predicts his demise, as well as, most importantly, providing him with a past. During the seven minutes that the scene lasts, we share with Billy an experience of time as he drinks vodka and describes his isolation. We feel we are there with him, the duration of the scene contributing to the atmosphere and to the rhythm of his life.

Billy from *The Road – A Story of Life and Death* (2013)

Peggy's death was an altogether lighter occasion because she lived a fulfilled life, having come to terms with both the death of her mother in the Holocaust and a problematic marriage. I am aware that Monty from *All White in Barking* passed away in 2014, and that a man I knew only as John, who appeared in *Lift*, committed suicide in the same year as the film's release. As he describes it in the film, he suffered from paranoid schizophrenia after the death of his parents. Such experiences serve as a stark reminder of the sensitivity and fragility entailed in filming the lives of real people.

The Character Ensemble

I recently produced a four-screen video installation (*Out of Time*, 2017) in which one of the pieces, *Moments of Silence*, features thirty-one characters from my previous films locked in specific reflective pauses. The idea came about after thinking for some time about how all the people I have filmed over the years could almost migrate or exchange places from one film to another because they share similar struggles and challenges. Some of them even look similar. The work is the most extreme example of an ensemble piece that I have produced but, since *Lift, I* have always found that the ensemble offers me the aesthetic and thematic freedom I crave.

My films focus on the relationship between character and the specific place in which the narrative unfolds. These places are both real and metaphorical spaces and I need to be free to paint a complete picture. A single-character-led story could never satisfy this desire. By choosing to film what usually amounts to four or five principal characters (and a small number of one-off scenes, as discussed previously), I am free to explore my chosen subject from a multitude of contrasting and complex perspectives and I hope, thereby, that the film will become greater than the sum of its parts.

Once a specific setting for a film has been decided, the casting possibilities are, of course, endless. In a film of sixty to seventy-five minutes it is better not to include more than four or five main characters if any real depth is to be achieved. When I begin filming with one or two characters that I've found interesting, a picture starts to slowly emerge and it becomes easier to decide whom else to look for to complete the ensemble. Each character must provide something different. But this is never an exercise in satisfying a preconceived notion or a sociological fit. In shooting the films, I have sometimes found myself finishing an individual character story before starting another, and at other times balancing the simultaneous filming of several of them over a prolonged period. It can be challenging to hold all of these unfolding stories in my head, so more often than not I find myself writing complex notes that form the basis of a rough script as I go along. This script serves only as an aid to stop me losing control of the process. When editing starts, I disregard it completely and, what's more, the editor will never see it. I usually have an instinctive feeling, when I have enough material for each character, that now's the time to start editing; but this process always entails a degree of uncertainty.

I approach the filming of the stories on a scene-by-scene basis, each one developing and deepening the story. But again, the order often changes during the editing. If you were to pick any one of the main-character stories in my films you would find that it's usually told in six or so scenes, together amounting to approximately ten to fifteen minutes of the film. As can be seen in *Calais: The Last Border*, *Men of the City* and *All White in Barking*, characters sometimes cross paths or interact in scenes, but this only occurs for solid narrative reasons and to enhance the construction of place.

Editing multiple character stories in a single film is a real joy. When the juxtapositions work, the films come alive and new ideas are created. I think of the creation of the ensemble as a mosaic which offers the viewer a dynamic and multifaceted picture of my chosen 'world'. I can still recall my amazement when I first discovered the principle of crosscutting between characters in an early documentary film that I assisted on, and I can still feel the excitement when I first watched Robert Altman's 1993 film, *Short Cuts*. I recently read Sherwood Anderson's 1919 novel, *Winesburgh, Ohio* - a novel that consists of 22 character stories in a single setting - and was again reminded of my attraction to this approach to storytelling.

Chapter Four

A Sense of Place

The construction of character in my work occurs alongside the construction of setting, the two elements wedded to each other in essential ways. In fact, the specific setting of a film, and its associated meaning, is usually the starting point for everything that follows. Before I commit to a specific setting, I have to be convinced that it can provide the film with a potent visual quality that will enhance the themes being explored. As with the characters themselves, the settings don't have to be exotic or remarkable but they must augment the lives of the people I have chosen to explore.

The process of constructing setting is again one of distillation. The Calais in my film, *Calais: The Last Border*, for example, bears little resemblance to the 'real' Calais. You can, of course, glimpse familiar locations and feel some of the atmosphere, but the film heavily manipulates reality to achieve its ends. You'll notice that each character in the film occupies a distinct physical space in the town: Ijaz - the industrial wasteland around the port; Tulia - the town centre and her home; Paul - the Channel Tunnel entrance area; and Steve - the Zoo Bar.

I chose to film in Calais precisely because it offered me the possibility to express and explore the struggles of people searching for a better life. This theme shaped the visual conception of the film and led me to think very specifically about the use of locations. For example, I spent many weeks searching for characters in and around the Channel Tunnel entrance before I finally encountered Paul. I knew the setting was strong and that I just had to be patient and wait for the right character to show up. Paul is only ever filmed in this single location, until the very last scene when he leaves to spend the night in a local bed-and-breakfast.

In this environment there were certain inbuilt filmic opportunities, such as the constant presence of English day-trippers, the bricked-up Eurostar ticket office, and other migrants stuck in the same predicament as Paul. Of course, I got lucky when Ernesta, the Lithuanian woman, appeared and I could build a scene around this encounter. But it was my decision to limit myself to the setting that enabled our chance meeting to occur. Similarly, by filming Ijaz solely in the port area of the town it was possible to make his story more claustrophobic and intense. And by filming Steve almost entirely in his bar I could broaden the theme of the search for a better life to include the perspective of somebody who had rejected the UK - the dream destination for both Paul and Ijaz – only to find himself 'trapped' in a different way.

Thwarted dreams, the hope for something better around the corner, and the desire to free oneself from one's past characterised Tulia's narrative. However, given that she was settled in Calais and had a business there, it was more challenging to find a distinct setting for her story. So I confined the action to her home and the site of her business operations. Her childhood experience of being a refugee positioned her firmly at the centre of the film and I enhanced her story by using images of the refugees currently in the town and of Ijaz stranded on the beach.

When I became committed to making a film about first love, the search for a suitable location governed much of the early research process. I could only imagine the film being set in an isolated rural setting where a sparse landscape would provide a meaningful backdrop, bringing into sharper focus the struggles of the young protagonists. Occasionally, one stumbles across settings for films by chance. This was the case with Siddick in Cumbria where Laura Anne's search for a 'prince' unfolds in *Someday My Prince Will Come* (2005). Again, the specifics of the setting determined the character of the film: the constant churning of windmills suggesting the relentless daily grind; the passage of the seasons mirroring the changing nature of the children; and the post-industrial landscape providing a constant reminder of lives lived against the odds.

Someday My Prince Will Come (2005)

I have been inspired by poets, filmmakers and painters when thinking about setting and am always interested in exploring the psychological effect a setting can have on the audience's reading of a film. I remember when I first encountered the work of the early 20th century Danish painter, Laurits Anderson Ring, how struck I was by the relationship of character to place. Most of his paintings show village life in southern Zealand. He infuses this landscape with an otherworldly mystique and strange mixtures of mood. Many of the works depict crossings and thresholds: the space between waiting and leaving in a doorway, at a window or a railroad crossing. The images also deal with transience and reflection and I often imagine myself asking the characters questions just as I do in my films.

At the Old House by Laurits Andersen Ring (1925)

In my kind of filmmaking, it is not always possible to exert total control over the construction of place and I would never refrain from shooting a scene in an 'imperfect' location if it means otherwise missing an opportunity to attain a greater insight into a character. In *All White in Barking* the setting wasn't particularly distinctive so I had to consider alternative ways of using visual metaphor in creating the character of the town. Also, unlike the people in *Calais: The Last Border*, the protagonists were physically settled and therefore many of the scenes unfolded within an interior domestic setting. Despite this, there were numerous possibilities that allowed for the creation of a strong sense of place. When I discovered the market trader selling cheap meat to desperate customers, I committed a lot of time to filming it, knowing it would benefit the film. This was also the case when I learned that the Labour club was being demolished.

There are many other examples of such metaphorical scenes in my films. In *The Road – A Story of Life and Death* we dip into a bingo hall to explore notions of chance and luck, experience a Shiite religious ceremony to reflect upon home and belonging, and enter a Somali café for similar reasons. Often these scenes also afford a brief exploration of character, as in *All White in Barking* in which a group of line-dancers reveal their feelings about immigration. Sometimes these scenes can also reappear throughout a film, like the chip van in *Calais: The Last Border*, in which the thoughts of the English day-trippers deepen and change in tandem with the broader narrative of the film.

About one year into the making of *Men of the City*, I was filming Steve, the street sweeper, at a demonstration against the 2008 financial crisis. On the way home I encountered two men arguing at a bus stop. One was homeless and the other a protestor. I was struck by the tone and apocalyptic theme of their conversation and so I stopped and filmed it. It was an isolated scene and I had no intention of following up on the men so I just forgot about it until the editing of the film began some months later. When my editor watched the rushes, he was also intrigued by this random encounter. It therefore ended up being the first dialogue scene of the film, precisely because it aided the construction, later in the film, of a distinct visual world featuring such parable-like elements as rain, floods and a rainbow. When a trader reveals his passion for deer hunting, it allows for a radical stylistic change of direction which reaches its climax in a later sequence when a man reveals that he once saved a woman from drowning in the River Thames. These one-off, sometimes heavily researched but occasionally spontaneous documentary moments aren't directly tied to the narrative of the films' central protagonists. But they are nevertheless extremely important in enabling poignant digressions that deepen the characterisation of a place and its associated themes whilst strengthening the overall atmosphere of the films. In addition to the construction of the setting and the use of metaphorical scenes, motifs are also deployed to give the films a greater resonance. Such motifs include meat in *All White in Barking*, borders and barriers in *Calais: The Last Border*, lights in *The Road – A Story of Life and Death*, and rain in *Men of the City*.

Chapter Five

My Short Films

After making *Lift* in 2001 I concentrated on making mid-length and feature-length films and it wasn't until 2011 that I made another short piece. Since then I have made an additional six. This is slightly odd, given that most filmmakers tend to concentrate on making short-form films at the beginning of their careers. This development, which has come as something of a surprise to me, is largely due to the growth of on-line platforms. It took me many years to come to terms with the fact that audiences can watch my work on a computer screen, so it wasn't until 2009 that I agreed to place *Lift* on YouTube. Now I am quite excited about the possibilities that on-line publication of films affords, simply because it is a way of circumventing the increasing demands of funders when considering projects involving large budgets. The problem of funding hasn't gone away, of course, but there is a lot that can be achieved for little cost and without unwanted interference.

I find the potential for conceptual and structural simplicity that the short form allows extremely interesting. In many of my short films, I have often attempted to work within the constraints of Aristotle's three unities - of action, place and time - as described in his *Poetics*. I have often confined the action to a single physical setting without the need to artificially combine different locations through editing; attempted to construct the narrative over a notional single day; and followed one central story with minimal sub-plots.

For example, in *The Old Man and His Bed* (2011) the story unfolds over the course of a single night and we never leave the space of the main protagonist's bedroom. Everything I deem important to communicate about the life of Bob, the old man, can be experienced within the confines of this space.

Similarly, *Sisters* (2017) unfolds in the single setting of a pub during one night. I actually shot *Sisters* in 2004 but it wasn't edited until 2017. Over the years I thought many times about editing the material but, due to other commissioned film work taking priority, the film was always put on the back burner. A student I was tutoring from the National Film and Television School had initially told me about the sisters, and one evening in 2004 a small group of us went to the pub they frequented in

London's St John's Wood. We filmed them for about three hours. I set myself the task of trying to express as much as possible without words and explanation, using as few shots as possible. The sisters expected me to ask questions but the questions never came. This method created an interesting tension, which I think you can sense on screen. Whilst editing the material, I was interested in how far I could push the silences and the sense of 'nothing happening' in the hope that viewers would experience their own sense of time unfolding and be stimulated to wonder about the lives of the sisters, with the minimum of direction from myself.

Bob from *The Old Man and His Bed* (2011)

In *Outsiders* (2014) I positioned myself inside a mobile food van located on a lay-by in rural Lincolnshire, looking out onto a field of cabbages. The food van didn't actually exist in this location but by manipulating its physical position I was able to create a meaningful aesthetic 'stage' on which the action could unfold.

The (mainly) British people who approach the van (and therefore the camera) enter onto this 'stage', their often xenophobic dialogues/actions driving the 'narrative' of the film. Meanwhile, scenes depicting migrants silently picking vegetables in the freezing fields provide a dramatic counterpoint, whilst also serving as transitions – or 'set changes' - that allow for the passing of time. The film encourages a reflection on the meaning of place, placement and displacement (the 'settled' Brits versus the migrants) whilst also preserving a strong sense of the unity of time and space by controlling the actuality during both shooting and post-production.

The interventions I made in this short film extended beyond creating a 'stage'. Many of the film's protagonists were cast in the local town and brought to the location for filming. They were chosen (where possible) for their articulate patterns of speech, with a view to enhancing the 'theatricality' of the film. By constricting time and space, the film elongates the time we spend with people in the location, thus creating depth through economy.

In *When Night Falls* (2016) I was again concerned with discovering how self-imposed formal constraints, when constructing mise-en-scène, could enhance the themes I was drawn to. By filming the protagonists strictly within the confines of their cabin abode as they bed down for the night, a specific triangular relationship based on proximity and intimacy was formed between the subjects, myself, and the viewer. By encouraging the protagonists to reveal their private lives and associated vulnerabilities, I intentionally played with existing perceptions of masculinity. Again, I eschewed traditional notions of the 'non-interfering' documentary observer, preferring, through a manipulated construction of time and space, to physically and thematically unify what was, in reality, a disparate ensemble of characters.

In *Touched by Murder* (2016) the body of a young Polish woman found in a London canal is the starting point of the film. By rejecting the approach documentary films normally adopt when dealing with the subject of murder (in this case by not positing the murder story as the main event) I looked into a suitable method of provocation designed to create a reflection on some of the most pertinent sub-themes suggested by the murder, such as urban disconnection, alienation, and our relationship to the 'stranger' among us.

Touched by Murder actively tests and develops the notion of *provocation* in the documentary film, to discover its storytelling potential and how it can shape and determine the filmic form of a work. By seeking out and engaging protagonists who had no direct relation to the murder victim, I tried to create an alternative story about specific reactions to the event. The film also reflects on how serendipity and chance can be deployed in the creation of a film poetic. It was a matter of chance that the body of the young woman floated down the canal and ended up outside a housing block (which then becomes the film's principal location). The opening sequences of the film are designed, by means of various conversations, to create the impression of normal lives disturbed by the murder. This is then taken further when, in the final sequence of the film, the protagonists are looking at a photograph of the young woman and her partner (the future murderer). By doing so, the film expands upon the verbal/conversational reactions to the murder because now, since no words are spoken, we are encouraged to focus on facial gestures. It isn't until the final shot that the photograph is seen by viewers - a decision taken to provoke them to directly experience for themselves their personal reactions to the incident.

Notes on Bangladesh (2017) had a very different genesis from my other shorts, and consequently, a very different narrative form. Like *Sisters*, the unedited rushes had been lying around in a box on a shelf for many years. The material was actually filmed in 2007 after I was invited by a French production company to make an 'ethnographic' film about anything anywhere in the world. They had received development funds from Arte Television and the Musée de l'Homme in Paris to make a collection of such films. I originally thought about filming in the remote tribal areas of India but for various pragmatic reasons ended up in Bangladesh on the Char, islands in the Ganges Delta that suffer severe flooding during the monsoon rains.

I undertook a twenty-five day research trip to find characters and locations, prior to my return for a 3-month filming period the following year. During this trip, I filmed twelve hours of 'research notes' on a small Sony camera. I never returned to make the film because the funding fell through. These notes therefore became the film. The presence of the human face and the sense of waiting permeate the film and, of course, the passage of time is a distinct feature.

I had never made a film so far from home amongst people whose reality was so different from my own. I understood little or nothing of what they expressed on camera and was left to focus on gestures and body language to get by. I was constantly questioning my motivation in a way that I never usually do and I decided to leave this ambiguity in the final edited version of the film.

Chapter Six

Reflections by Collaborators

There are a number of key collaborators with whom I have worked over the years. Three of them, David Charap (Film Editor), Rachel Wexler (Producer) and Michel Duvoisin (Composer), have made substantial contributions to most of my films. There is also a small group of researchers who have played key roles in the making of the films. I invited them all to offer an insight into the filmmaking process from the very different perspectives that their unique roles afford.

David Charap – Film Editor

Since we meet fairly frequently I have a better idea of what Marc's films are about, before we start the edit, than most projects I work on. It is very different being confronted with real filmed faces and places than whatever preconceptions I might have from a conversation or outline treatment. My initial impressions as I start labelling material and assigning it to separate folders are very important. I am able to react spontaneously to what Marc has presented me with, and just for a brief spell I am not worrying about how it will cut together or how it should be structured. When something strikes me during this phase it is likely to remain a feature of the edit. I remember seeing Ijaz trying on the hats in *Calais*, knowing that this was a character to fall in love with and that Marc's relationship with him would be the core of the film. The dying Billy from *The Road*, with a light bulb for company, was always going to be the heart of the film, right from the first rushes.

Almost instinctively the next step is to keep an eye open for beginnings and endings. This can be within a scene, when something interesting starts happening, or a moment when it all starts feeling dull, but it is also thinking: When does a character's story begin and where does it take you? In Marc's work this is usually chronological, as he gets to know a character better as their story unfolds, but sometimes story beats come in a different order and that is where I need to start.

Part of the joy of an edit is discovering what I'm doing as I'm going along. I think I have a good grasp of what intrigues Marc and know that he prefers films that suggest their themes rather than state them explicitly, so that the viewer is complicit in constructing the film's meaning. So, *Men of the City* never says that the City is a dehumanising environment that puts its citizens at peril of their souls, but I knew that was the sort of idea Marc had playing around in his head. When Marc presented chance encounters - like the man rescuing a woman drowning or the bus stop duo discussing dogs' souls - I felt emboldened to push quite stylised techniques in the edit to give the film an epic quality rather than just being observational.

A lot of editing is pragmatic - how do you get from A to B with no cutaways? When Marc told me that in *Calais* he was interested in how characters' stories relate to one another, I saw an opportunity to use images of Ijaz to cut with Tulia's back-story. It is also a question of making something out of what you have. When Marc complained that Fakhrul, the Bengali sign holder in *Men of the City*, wasn't forthcoming about what he was thinking but that rushes existed from another project in Bangladesh, I thought maybe there would be something to give us an insight into what he was thinking. Hence cows falling in the river! Totally spurious, of course, but somehow expressing a filmic truth that neither of us could have anticipated.

It is very strange meeting an actor on a film I have edited. They've never heard of me, yet I may have spent three months listening to their voice and examining every nuance of their facial expressions. It is even worse with Marc's documentaries. There is a disconnect, however, between the real person and the character I know on the screen. Like Marc, I have to manipulate what the camera records to express some kernel of truth or insight, irrespective of what happens in the rest of their lives outside the frame. Sometimes this is frustrating - why can't they just say what I know they mean more succinctly? Why do they have to refer to spurious details that mean we will have to cut and splice what they are saying? But over time in the cutting room I come to relish their idiosyncrasies and enjoy how reliably they repeat the same words and actions in their material as they did when I first met them in the rushes. This doesn't help make sense of their stories, however. I don't have to relate to them in the same way Marc does, it's more a matter of understanding what their role is in the film. Why has Marc chosen them? Where does the material take you?

To construct their narrative I rely on my intuition about what is an arresting way to meet them and what is an appropriate way to leave them. Then it is truly a question of filling in the gaps as elegantly as possible. The editing process then involves probing the material and discovering what you can discard, or sometimes what you still urgently need - which is why it is helpful if filmmakers hold back a couple of shooting days until late in the edit.

The great advantage of multiple-character stories is that when one narrative reaches a suitable turning point you can break away, cut to someone else whose story is now illuminated by the sequence you have just left, and you can resume the first story whenever it suits without having to explain what has happened in between. Most single-character stories do not have this luxury. You face the challenge of sustaining a character's story when a viewer may be yearning for a break, change or space to process what they are watching. I love the fact that in Marc's ensemble films a set of small stories adds up to something more profound - the whole is very much more than the sum of its parts. This feels very close to what editing is about in its most fundamental sense. It also applies to a single-character story. But I fear that a fully rounded portrait is easier to dismiss as a special case, whereas a collection of stories tends to create a film as a parable that lingers in the mind. I think we have both been surprised at how much emotional baggage and varied personal responses viewers will bring to a film even if the filmmakers assume they have been very clear and direct about what they are trying to say. It seems to me much more satisfying to guide viewers rather than instruct or tell them what to think. As someone once put it, you can invite them to a meal and prepare the dishes but you don't want to have to do the eating for them. This isn't an excuse for lazy thinking or lack of rigour in the edit. But the more clearly the editor can identify and isolate the themes that interest the director, the richer the viewers' responses are likely to be.

Compression of time is obviously one of the key features of what editing does. Yet simply assembling an hour of the best bits of footage that may have been recorded over several months throws up real challenges in storytelling to convey the passage of time. 'Years passed and nothing interesting happened' is just about acceptable on the page but demands something special to work on screen. Being sparse with music can help. Establishing recurring motifs may work - like the chip shop in *Calais*.

One striking thing I have learned in the cutting room is how profound our sense of time is linked to the sun. A film that is punctuated by night shots feels more substantial than one without. Glimpses of sunset or sunrise instantly convey time passing, and different seasons even more so. Construction of space is less problematic, I feel, in the edit. The viewer simply accepts what they are presented with, unless given cause for suspicion. So interiors filmed in a studio can be made to feel like they belong to an exterior without a huge amount of effort. If you cut from a shot of someone looking out of a window to a wide-shot of a cityscape, the chances are that we'll believe we are seeing what they are looking at even if the two shots were recorded in widely different places at different times.

What is perhaps more tricky in Marc's work is when the space itself becomes the object of examination. So in *Lift* the space is what defines the film. I fear both *Calais* and *The Road* are less successful in defining the space they are nominally 'about' because the space itself is quite big and amorphous. It helps if there are distinctive landmarks that define the world of the film. This is true in fiction films as well.

Michel Duvoisin – Composer

What I am about to write, describing some moments over the 16 years Marc and I have been working together, is in some ways, a reflection on the invention of working together as a team, both with Marc and also with David (Editor). When I worked on *Travellers*, my first film with Marc, we were constantly bouncing ideas back and forth about where music should be and where it shouldn't be. What struck me most about the film, in musical terms, was not just the sense of travel but also not knowing where the characters' journeys and film narrative would lead. This was the first time that Marc had used music in a film and I was aware that it was a new experience for him. The piece that means most to me is the one accompanying Caroline's story and I developed it to appear in various forms; for example, the hospital scene in which Dave, the elderly man, visits his wife.

In many of the films we have made together, we have come up with musical themes for individual characters but there are also pieces that are the 'voice of the film'. These pieces glue the different character narratives together and emphasize the sense of a common journey. A moment that sticks out in my mind is from *Men of the City* when Steve, the street sweeper (who I think is the happiest of our three main protagonists), looks down over the financial district of London and is linked musically to the plight of Norman, the insurance salesman, who finds a release from the strains of his work by driving through the forest on his motorbike. The same music also links David, the hedge fund manager, who is filmed in his plush apartment adorning the walls with enormous photographic prints of his children. Through the creation of a musical connectivity, we come to understand how each person is not so different.

I've also learned as a film composer working on documentaries that music shouldn't impose itself too much on the viewer. Marc usually insists that the music appears in scenes in a very subtle way to enhance the mood, and often it can be most effective when you don't overtly notice its presence. From the point of view of the composer it can be quite a challenge to strike the correct balance. How do you write something that doesn't take over the scene? It's a very different approach from a film like *Star Wars,* for example, where the original film was very flat until John Williams came on board.

Technically speaking, the first films with Marc were guitar-based, which I felt comfortable with. But then, when we made *Calais: The Last Border,* I was shaken out of my comfort zone and had to learn how to play the accordion. And this is what I love most about the process. Just as Marc meets people who are strangers, I sometimes meet instruments that are strangers too and over time we become familiar with each other. Whether I play violin or end up playing trumpet or sitar, there are always new sounds that emerge.

Rachel Wexler – Producer

I originally met Marc whilst we were both working at a TV production company where I was a production manager and he was directing his first film, *Lift.* I really enjoyed talking with him and Russell Crockett (Editor) about the project and spending time watching the ongoing edit. I realised he had a unique way of filming with his contributors and a wonderful style that I hadn't experienced before.

After that first encounter, we used to bump into each other at festivals and events and, in 2003 at the festival (IDFA) in Amsterdam, we had a drink together and shared our frustrations about working for other people and our hopes to one day have more filmmaking autonomy. We were both fans of the BBC's Storyville strand and had both spent time with Nick Fraser, and I recall we decided to see if we could maybe find a film together to make for Nick.

Someday My Prince Will Come (2005)

In 2004, when I employed a new cleaner through an agency, a woman with a headscarf came to the house. She seemed distracted and we started talking. I immediately liked her and I felt she wanted to talk. We had a cup of coffee and chatted. The next time she came to the house we spoke again and she revealed that she was actually one of seven 'wives' living with a Messianic rabbi and had been banished by him from the family home. She was very distressed that she'd had to leave her little girl with the family. I told her that I was a documentary producer and that I was Jewish too... and that my friend Marc and I would love to visit the family and would she introduce us? She soon made contact with Philip, the Rabbi, who invited Marc and me to their home. That was the start of a long period of trust-building with Philip. Marc made himself vulnerable to Philip, which he liked, and he didn't judge him, at least not visibly.

We spoke for hours about this man and I love the fact that Marc used me as one of his sounding boards and shared his inner thoughts. I think it's an incredibly important part of the creative process and one that is both fruitful and really enjoyable. The most thrilling part of producing a film is when you know that it's actually going to get made, that all of the hard work developing the story, meeting the contributors and honing the idea has successfully been translated and understood by your funding partners and they are going to support you in making it happen. The relationship completely changes from being on separate sides of a table to joining together and all investing in making a piece of work that will hopefully find an audience and be something we can feel proud of.

One of the most valuable parts of the process of working with Marc creatively is learning about the contributors he's found and their unique life stories. He goes very deep with his contributors. Like Marc, I am also drawn to the process of understanding ourselves as humans through hearing about the stories of others. It's what drew me into documentaries in the first place.

One of the most exciting parts of making a film with Marc is going into the edit to see the rough cut. I've usually seen early footage of the contributors and then have heard ongoing filming reports. But apart from that I've not been into the edit much at all. That way I'm hopefully one of the early viewers who can give a reaction to the film and give feedback. We would also usually have our main funder – mostly Nick Fraser – in the viewing too. There is always some trepidation in showing the first cut to a commissioning editor but Nick has always been hugely supportive and engaged (apart from one time that he'd just come off the Red Eye flight from New York and he fell asleep... Coffee and cake revived him and we carried on).

Selling films is a constantly changing job. I believe that, inherently, TV is fickle and sadly quite predictable in what is shown. Unfortunately, many films that would find a large and engaged audience don't get made because they don't have a conventional 'hook' or storyline. This makes finance- raising and selling human-interest stories, which play out thematically rather than with a conventional narrative, very hard. We have succeeded whenever the commissioning editor watches Marc's early footage and understands the very layered and subtle nature of the work. This kind of film is very popular with audiences, though, and I try and push through the boundaries by finding key patrons.

When speaking with buyers about Marc's work, I often find myself starting with discussing his approach and the painstaking and dedicated way that he finds the contributors. There is often some kind of geographical or societal way in to the films – as in *The City*, or *Barking* – and that is a starting point to raise interest in the idea. I then grab their attention by telling them about the characters and their often extraordinary lives. The depth of Marc's affection and care for the contributors shines through in these conversations. I think it really helps that I become completely smitten with the contributors and their stories through his footage, and if I am passionate about their stories then it can become infectious to the listener. But it can also just leave them cold... It depends on their compassion and sensibilities. You can't please everyone!

We've been able to work with self-determination and a lot of freedom. Marc is completely focussed, authentic, and dedicated to his films and the contributors in a way that's really special. I know that the best partners in any creative endeavour are the ones who love the project as much as you do and are emotionally invested. Producing is incredibly frustrating at times but working with talented and close partners makes the whole experience much more rewarding. Not to be too sentimental but I do think of Marc as my documentary brother and hope that we'll continue to find a way to collaborate until we're too old to do it any more.

Guy King - Assistant Producer

For Marc it's a bit like the early stages of writing a novel, I imagine, with the same painstaking commitment of a writer locked away in a shed for a year. He patiently and obsessively seeks out characters that wouldn't be out of place in a good novel: well-drawn, good-humoured, unselfconscious, anguished and loveable. Whereas the novelist will crunch up hundreds of parchments and toss them in the bin, Marc and his researchers occupy hundreds of cafés, street corners and places of work, eyes peeled. He puts his entire development budget into researchers – often, young ones who are affordable and motivated. Motivated, because talking to complete strangers on the street is one of the hardest parts of the process. It's creative work and really fun, but it takes ferret-like tenacity and hunting-dog enthusiasm. Turning over stones, panning for gold. Only by holding his nerve as a director, and waiting and waiting until the right characters are discovered, will he then meet them and think about filming. Marc prefers to be surprised rather than find exactly what he is looking for, although when we researched the financial district it was uncanny how we found some real-life examples of types we had imagined: a sandwich-board holder, hedge fund manager, cigar-smoking broker in pinstripes.

Marc puts more emphasis on character than story and is confident that a strong character inherently carries an interesting story. I was aware from the beginning that their spirit had to overlap somehow with his own but I could only present him with possibilities – then the decision is his.

When researching *Men of the City,* we'd taken inspiration from the children's book *Momo* by Michael Ende, in which a street kid exposes the malevolent 'men in grey suits' with the help of a philosophical road-sweeper. I met about 30 road-sweepers in and around Bank and Liverpool Street. In fact, there was one woman we did a bit of filming with, before the film became more about the *men* of the city. The 31st road-sweeper I spoke to was Steve. He pulled out of his dustcart a manuscript entitled 'A Treatise on Descartes'. He'd written his own criticism of French philosophy and was hoping to publish it. We'd found our philosophical road-sweeper! Luckily Marc related to him too.

Marc is drawn to foreigners, of course, and charismatic working-class East Enders. When I met his parents, this fell into place. His dad is a big loveable Cockney taxi driver who loves football and the grandkids. His mum couldn't be any sweeter and wouldn't be out of place in a lift in Whitechapel. And as English as they are, they are Russian Jewish too.

Marc's relationship with people on-camera is obviously the most important bit. It all begins off-camera, where he expertly avoids the human urge to connect with people and make them feel at ease. It is important they are relaxed, to an extent, but keeping some taut energy is also important - some uneasiness, suspicion, slight discomfort, edge. Because when this translates through the lens it touches something deep inside the audience. Deep anxieties, frustrations, fears – universal anguish. Then your questions stoke the fire, not in a friendly or unfriendly way but timelessly, like an alien landed in London wondering what humans are up to. What are they doing? Really *doing*? I understand the need for all of this, so my relationship with them is about facilitating this.

Because I'm working behind the scenes I know that the people taking part are having a great time, even if they appear edgy. Some people enjoy being asked difficult questions, and we've spent many months finding those people. Ultimately, Marc is compassionate and respectful but in the early scenes he creates a tension that is necessary to the story. It's an act, a form of play, part of the performance, to create 'straitened circumstances', to use a phrase the critic AA Gill used in reference to *Outside the Court*. Some discomfort for the audience is probably a good thing because I know that, for all the characters we were working with, they weren't uncomfortable with us.

When I hear someone say they found one of Marc's films uncomfortable to watch, I'm upset. But I'm the sort of person who wants everyone to be happy so I'll find any form of criticism hard to take. Marc is more relaxed about the variety of responses he gets. Some directors might feel uncomfortable in that position. Personally, I love the taut revealing moments he creates. Art should make you shift in your seat a bit. It's enjoyable to shift on your cinema seat.

Marc is a bit mischievous, a proud agitator, but ultimately indebted to, enamoured by, and respected by his 'actors'. He never has an unkind word to say about any of the people he films with – and they can feel that. They enjoy having their portraits drawn - they find value in this sort of exploration of their characters. They intuitively have to believe in the film and to have a robustness of self. And that all goes back to the beginning of the process and spending achingly long hours finding the right characters in the first place.

When we filmed Bob from the film *The Old Man and His Bed,* we slept in sleeping bags in his living room, waiting through the night until he needed the toilet. Marc decided that the only time we could understand emphysema was on his daily trip to the lavatory carrying his oxygen tank, a journey that took Bob to the point of horribly gasping for breath. This sort of filming is only possible with characters that I'd got to know intimately, who trusted us. I looked back at some of my notes on Bob. It was a short seven-minute film but I had pages of notes. This sort of thing: 'Bob says his life has been taken away, he feels shelved on his way to the next place. He says he is in a reflective solitary place that would be like purgatory if he wasn't protected by his happiness. He is going through a period of unlearning because things are giving up on him: holding things, doing things. It's the opposite of being a child, who is able to learn things. He imagines the astronauts in space with their oxygen tanks and how they must arrive back on earth and take a big gasp of air. He used to love American cigarette boxes, the flavours, the stylish colours. He really loved smoking, the way you would bring your hand to your mouth, the inhalation, everything about it. He started to smoke aged 10. He remembers a number of road direction signs through his life and at those turnings he would always turn the wrong way. He hopes to beat the illness. Even though it is terminal. Historical trends of Oxygen levels in air were 35% back when there were dinosaurs, now big cities like London rarely see above 19%. At night, photosynthesis is not occurring so oxygen is not being created.' Marc replied in an email: 'Then we should film in the middle of the night.'

I've always felt Marc is creating art that will survive and that his tender, raw space is what's created in those few feet between his lens and the actor's nose – a magic vacuum in which oxymoronic emotion exists: humorous woe, confident fallibility, street philosophy.

Juliet Joffe – Assistant Producer

Little did I know, when I started working as a researcher on *The Road – A Story of Life and Death* that this journey would stay with me as a deeply formative and inspiring experience. The job of researching the characters was a fascinating one in many ways. Marc gave me a lot of freedom whilst clearly expressing his sensitivity, which he probably knew I could relate to in the first place. The approach of not setting in stone a structure or specific characters early in the process, allowing for surprises and organic development through time, has become very dear to me now as a filmmaker myself.

Many directors don't allow themselves this realm of possibilities when they embark on a new film, partly because being very open is daunting - who knows where the research will lead? But also because funders often require the filmmaker to know exactly who, when, and where they are going to film before the process has started, as well as wanting a clearly defined dramaturgy. Obviously this is asking for the process in reverse - who can predict what people will do? It encourages documentary makers to choose stories that are more predictable, safer or one-dimensional.

Making *The Road – A Story of Life and Death* was a real adventure, both on an artistic and human level. We were very free to explore different possibilities and to discuss them with Marc, shaping and reshaping possible narratives. Walking up and down the road, sometimes full of energy, sometimes exhausted and lost, I would always remember Marc's words: 'Just be open to surprises.'

Georgina Cammalleri – Assistant Producer

During my walk along the road for the research in *The Road – A Story of Life and Death*, I spoke to everyone, from former communist Afghani soldiers and lonely Sudanese landlords to Jewish refugees, Irish musicians and exiled Persians. In the process I became their friends and, at times, something akin to their social worker or therapist.

Once, while we were having a coffee before filming a contributor, I remember Marc reading over my notes about a specific contributor and half whispering, half mumbling to himself, 'I'll ask her about this... then that... then that will lead onto this... which will then get us to that moment.' He was creating an emotional road map that would help him get to the core of that person's story.

Whilst 'on set' with Marc, I'd often find myself hidden in the most awkward of places – behind a door, behind a plant, in the next room - always making sure that I was within earshot but utterly invisible. I'd listen in carefully to Marc asking questions in a warm but direct tone. What I noticed was his ability to stay calm during awkward moments. Where another person would quickly laugh or speak to fill the silence, Marc would remain there like a pillar with his camera, just holding the shot and waiting. It gives an unnatural pace to the conversation, and an unnerving one at times, but it allows the contributor to think further. Rather than getting an answer and moving on, the pause gets the contributor thinking more deeply about the topic. Just when I'd think they'd finished making a point, there would be a long pause. I'd lean forward to see if they had finished, only to find Marc utterly still and holding his gaze on the contributor and suddenly there would be an afterthought. This process brought about some of the best lines, jokes and insights.

The most profound character relationship I had was with Billy, the Irishman in *The Road.* He didn't have many friends but was well-liked. We spent a lot of time together. One time he told me that he had received a letter from the hospital and that they wanted to see him. He wasn't sure whether to go or not – he often tried to avoid confronting his issues – but I insisted that he had to go. Then he turned to me and asked: 'Will you go with me?' I hesitated, then agreed I would. Although I am always mindful of letting the contributors understand that our relationship is one which exists within the bounds of the documentary, the reality is that you are dealing with people's secrets, dreams and, in essence, their whole life. This is why I believe Marc prefers to stay away from contributors between filming – it allows the interactions to remain fresh yet familiar; intimate but with enough distance to allow the asking of difficult questions and to not allow his feelings to cloud his vision - even if in the moment the interaction is a very emotional one.

Billy and I caught the tube together and headed to Chelsea and Westminster Hospital. The doctors began testing his heart while I sat in the waiting room. Then a friendly Welsh nurse popped his head in and called my name. He asked me into the clinical room where Billy lay there on his back, bare-chested, covered in electrodes. The nurse ushered me to the corner of the room. I explained I was a friend, that we came to know each other from working on a documentary about the lives of immigrants who settled on the A5 road but that I was one of a few people who was in regular contact with Billy. Saying all this aloud made me realise how hard it was to keep the boundaries in place.. At this point, the nurse became sombre and said to me: 'You know, Billy is a ticking time bomb.' I was hit with a deep sinking feeling of hopelessness. Later that day, Billy and I had lunch and I began my campaign to get him to reduce his alcohol intake. Christmas came and I left London to see my family. Billy left me a message wishing me a Merry Christmas. That was the last I heard of him.

When I returned, I remember Marc asked me to check on all the contributors and I went around calling and knocking on people's doors. I got no answer from Billy's number. I headed to his home and continued ringing. I could hear his phone ringing from the other side of the door but no one answered. I called the police and they broke into Billy's flat to find him there, dead. He had died of a heart attack. These moments are a stark reminder that, as documentary makers, we deal with life at its most intense but also fragile. I still think of Billy on a regular basis. The same goes for other contributors who feature in that particular film.

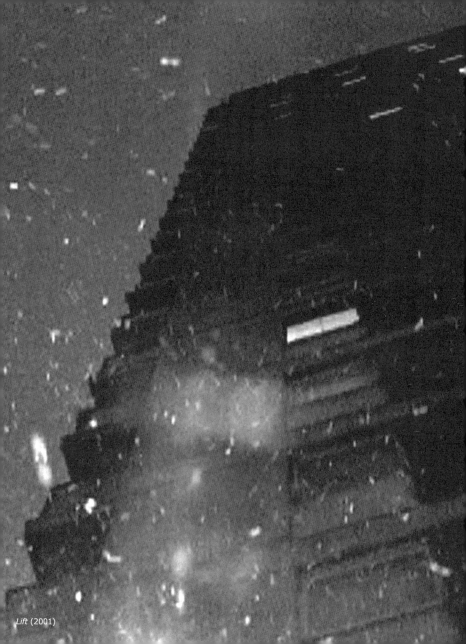

Lift (2001)

Chapter Seven

Essays

Lift, *Travellers*, and *Calais: The Last Border*
by Graeme Hobbs

Teeth of a digger bucket scrape the concrete, clearing the debris at the remains of the Sangatte refugee camp; wind blows through the lift shaft of a tower block as the cable mechanism whirrs into action; a crisscrossing of rails sways us into a station. All three of these films – *Calais: The Last Border*, *Lift*, *Travellers* – are based in transitional areas, pinch points, places through which people travel to go somewhere, or hope to. It is in these places that Isaacs sows questions that take people off-guard, reconnecting them with the deeper motivations and themes of their lives.

Travellers

'*We are all wounded inside in some way. We all carry unhappiness within us for some reason or other. Which is why we need a little gentleness and healing from one another.*'[1]

The idea behind *Travellers* – getting people to talk about their relationships and ideas of love in railway carriages and stations throughout the land resembles that of a classic British Transport Film promoting the unexpected benefits of train travel, a feeling enhanced by the shots of whooshing trains and platforms at sunset. But this is 2002, not 1952, and the storylines aren't so easily tidied up. Relationships are broken, and as well as tales of new connections made and old loves maintained, we hear of hurt, pain, abuse and bullying in people's lives. Throughout, people talk of love, its surge, and fear of its loss.

For all its unavoidably worn nature, though, there is an underlying idealism here for the possibilities of making connections, of reaching across to give succour, and of the redemptive possibilities of love. One man's incantation on the word runs throughout. As he shivers on a platform, his phrases punctuate the film: "*Without love we can't live together; without love we can't say hello to each other; without love we can't live peacefully: we need to sow love.*" It seems like he has been there forever, a crazy prophet, freezing at a nondescript station somewhere in England, sheltering from the wind in a plastic shelter on a mean yellow flip seat, and with words for us all to hear: *"We're travellers, you know, and all what we need in this world is love."*

As the trains traverse the country, past back yards and past the sea, through wooded cuttings and dark winter fields, the amount of travellers, the volume of their stories, and the possibilities for their connection, multiply into journeys of endless possibility.

Lift

"Hello. So you're in the lift – again. What motivates you to want to stand in lifts for 10 hours a day … tell me, why do you do this?"

The sudden hush that the closing of lift doors brings, enclosing familiar strangers in uncomfortable proximity, brings out the tics and twitches before speech, the eyes on the edge of fear, need or loneliness, the people ready with a defensive wall of humour. This film is not clinically prying, though, and comes instead from a place of genuine curiosity, and the project of seeding people's lives with words that may take root in their walls of daily inconsequence. We don't hear Isaacs' answer to the resident's question. Instead, we hear his own questions to those who share the confined space: *Are you in love? What's the best thing you remember about your childhood? What motivates you to get up in the morning?*

Passing though are the contented and the lonely, the hospitable, the jolly, the drunks and the chatterers, the concerned and the religious, the shy and the barely-glimpsed. Sometimes their answers are disarming in their simplicity: *Can you tell me what you were thinking about today?* "Oh, I'm just happy for it was a beautiful day. I was thinking about how great it is to be alive." *Are you serious?* The woman looks straight at the camera, and there is no doubt. "Very."

Snatches of stories are left hanging with the lift's arrival at the ground floor or at a person's home. As the residents grow accustomed to his presence, Isaacs continues these fractured existential conversations, or people pick up where they left off by amplifying their earlier statements. Others start saying why they are leaving the lift. After a drink one evening, one man lingers as the door closes, wanting to talk more, seeing the opportunity to continue the evening.

Calais: The Last Border

Calais pictures booze-tripping Brits, trolleys stacked with bottles of Black Tower and Blossom Hill, and would-be immigrants, hoping for asylum, safety and a better life in Britain. The attitudes of the English, voiced at the ketchup, chips and tea hut, match the wall of primary colours from the warehouse opposite, its bright yellow turning sulphurous with dusk. "They're just taking over the whole country, they're living in bloody luxury hotels." "They're demanding this and demanding that, at the expense of our own people." "Nobody likes to think there's going to be another Holocaust, or anything like that, but there has to be a cut-off point," says one woman, as her husband tries out a phrase or two in his best *It Ain't Half Hot, Mum* accent and a flock of gulls attacks a discarded carton of chips.

Their world is in marked contrast to the shades of blue-grey that characterize that of the asylum seekers and those refused entry to Britain. For them, the wind that blows through the fences and wires at the entrance to the Channel Tunnel is a cheerless, goading companion.

Morning prayers take place on a fenced wasteland to the wail of a police siren. "Please come in," says Ijaz to Isaacs later, inviting him through a metal gate into a puddly concrete and breeze-block goods yard of oil drums and rusting metal – improvised night shelters for the determined. Ijaz's family were killed in a rocket attack on Kabul. *How do you feel?* asks Isaacs. Ijaz laughs, as he often does. "It's a difficult question, sir … Sometime before, I lost my mother, my father, my sister, my brother, and now this time there's nobody with me, so I'm extremely sad. It's a very difficult time for me."

He walks between breakwaters on the blue-brown North Sea shoreline, a man in a duffle-coat under a ragged, lowering sky. As the film goes on, his optimism is gradually broken down to the point of tears.

Earlier, spoken by a woman off the booze coach: "Very lucky people, we say it every morning when we get up - aren't we the luckiest people in the world?"

Three Meals

A resident of the tower block walks into the lift with a blue plastic bag, determined to address this fellow with the camera who has taken up daily residence there. "How are you, you alright, yeah? You want to eat something? Banana? OK, take it, alright." Isaacs later pictures himself with his camera and the half-eaten banana. Offers of chips and betel nut follow.

A man is eating at the burger stand in Calais. "I don't like the asylum seekers because they sponge off the English government," he says, emphasizing his point with a thin, floppy chip. "I'm very sorry mate but if that's the way it is, it's the way it is." As he walks out of camera, he delivers his parting shot: "I'll tell you what, I'd shoot the fucking lot of them." An older man in the queue looks at the camera silently, the corner of his mouth moves very slightly, and it is impossible to tell with whom he is in unspoken sympathy.

Jamaican Paul, having arrived on a useless ticket two days after visa rules changed, sits at a scuffed grass snack area at a garage near the channel tunnel entrance, his bags on the bench behind him as he talks of his wish to show off Jamaican food and the meals he wanted to cook as a big-time chef in England: "Chicken soup, beef soup, red pea soup, oxtail, curry goat, fricassee chicken, French fried chicken, rice and peas, wild rice, dumpling and yam and banana." The film cuts to frying onions at the chip stall, their sound that of pouring rain.

Three Things

After a while, a resident recognises the existence of the man in their lift by donating a chair with a red plastic seat. "I see they've given you a chair," says a woman in a fleece hat, to which Isaacs responds, *What did you dream about last night?*

In Calais, Ijaz is given a blue Bic razor at a handout by Secours Catholique. In the adjoining Portakabin he asks Isaacs, behind the camera, "I would like to make you a shave – would you like?" He then adds, "We are preparing for London" before walking out fresh-faced into the morning.

Anne is in hospital. Eight months on from her stroke, her husband buys her flowers from a station kiosk, his hand resting on their cellophane as they sit on the seat next to him on his way to a visit. After a curt "In here" to Isaacs, he wakes her and gives her a kiss, the pressure between their hands an unspoken version of the marriage vow that we hear later at

Beverley and Tony's wedding: *all that I have I share with you, all that I am I give to you*. Earlier, Isaacs had asked him what it would be like without this love in his life. "I think I'd be done," he says.

Three Photographs

The first is of a man, whom Isaacs has never met, in his bath. "He'll kill me for this," says Beverley, showing him the photograph as she stands in their shared home. It's a testament to Isaacs' ability to tease out stories, but also to the readiness of people to honestly share their lives, however difficult, given the chance of conversation. "The love that I've got now, it's a love love. There's a difference," says Beverley.

A creased, edge-blackened photograph shows a smiling young girl with a buttoned-up coat and a bow in her hair. Tulia tells her story, and we learn she is herself an immigrant and that the photograph dates from around the time that she went searching for her mother, from whom she had been separated at their wartime internment camp in Spain; a photograph from before the time she decided that no child of hers would be born to live through such an experience.

What did your mother look like? asks Isaacs. Ijaz smiles. "She looked like me. You can see in my face that she looked like me." He is then asked if he has a photograph of her. "I came to France in very difficult ways, very dangerous ways. I had one picture of my mother but at the moment I don't have her picture, I'm sorry to say." Visions arrive of a hastily-vacated room, or confined space, a jettisoned holdall with items so precious they cannot be lost, but which are lost along the way. The last time we see Ijaz he is waiting for a meal at a soup kitchen. He says to Isaacs, "You must only pray for me, because I don't have anyone, I am alone."

Accommodation

Underlying all of these films is the theme of *accommodation*, the give and take of adjusting to and living with another's presence and needs, the acceptance of what can be given, what can be lost, and what can be shared, whether this is on the scale of a tower block or a country.

The films do not require neat endings; they leave us looking down roads and along railway lines, imagining the countless stories, of residents, of immigrants, of booze-trippers, of train passengers; travellers all.

At the outset I quoted Ben Okri, from his essay 'Beyond Words'. I'll end with his words too, this time from his collection of aphorisms, 'The Human Race is Not Yet Free', in which he asks what hope there is for individual realities in a world such as ours, dominated by forces of violence, orthodoxy and manipulation of public opinion. He concludes: 'The only hope is in daring to redream one's place in the world – a beautiful act of imagination, and a sustained act of self-becoming. Which is to say that in some way or another we breach and confound the accepted frontiers of things.'[2] These films are a small step in that direction. In *Travellers*, a train, aglow with golden light, crosses a bridge.

1. Ben Okri, 'Beyond Words', in *A Way of Being Free*, Phoenix House, London, 1997, p.89

2. Ben Okri, 'The Human Race is Not Yet Free', in *A Way of Being Free*, Phoenix House, London, 1997, p.55

Graeme Hobbs is a writer living in the Welsh borders. Some of his chapbooks can be seen at http://colvabooks.blogspot.com

Someday My Prince Will Come / Philip and His Seven Wives
by Nick Bradshaw

Home is where the heart wonders in this odd-couple pair of mid-naughties Marc Isaacs studies of gallant love seekers from the opposite ends of England, which fill in the gap in Second Run's Isaacs catalogue between his transit portraits *Lift* (2001), *Calais: The Last Border* (2003) and *Travellers* (2002) and his subsequent metropolitan cross sections *All White in Barki*ng (2008) and *Men of the City* (2009). The oppositions are fetching: *Someday My Prince Will Come* follows ten-year-old serial monogamist Laura-Anne through a year of haphazard relationships with sundry local boys from her windswept locale of Siddick, on the Cumbrian coast, as they verge on the pressures of adolescence; *Philip and His Seven Wives* shacks up with an erstwhile rabbi turned horse-rearer, secondhand-furniture magnate and polygamist in Hove as he attempts to chivvy all seven women towards his vision of the divine. But both approach their subjects without condescension or sensation, and indeed consider their struggles within frameworks of fanciful precociousness (Laura-Anne's scripted courtly rhyming couplets; Philip's God-revealed identity as a Scriptural king) that allow Isaacs to combine their subjectivity with deadpan irony.

"In Siddick, where men used to dig for coal...

Now it's just two little streets, and most men on the dole."

Playing out against the backdrop of Siddick's big, beckoning seascapes and its budding rows of busy wind turbines, Laura-Anne's romantic rondo serves as both a thumbnail rehearsal of the never-smooth course of love and a prism on life in a deindustrialised northern village. The child's-eye entry point to adult affairs is a common enough trope, but Isaacs never uses Laura-Anne to wink at the audience: an early doorstop conversation she has with Isaacs about kissing ("Err... tingly") establishes that she's no naïf, and her voiceover's encapsulation of her quest for a prince "to keep her warm, and light up her heart" reminds us that she's as entitled to her needs and dreams as any full-throated Disney princess.

Nor does Isaacs suffice to wring his hands at the poverty he finds in Siddick – plain as it is to see in the edges of his frame. Laura-Anne's cousin/ neighbour/sometime beau Stephen isn't a case study but a strange, formidable and vulnerable pre-teen whose mother says is now at a stage where he needs the influence of his (imprisoned) father. The image of this pint-sized Wild One shambling home across the village green with his school bag barely holding in place his half-buttoned shirt is a wonder of motivational mystery – is this a pose or genuine delinquency? A later conquest of Laura-Anne's, Jamie from "over the sea" (i.e. neighbouring Seaton), is more prematurely wizened – "Dad always used to hit us but it just made us harder," he says impassively, before stepping outside to suck on a cigarette and rehearse his smoke rings. We don't see the beating he claims he's just administered Ben, another of Laura-Anne's exes; for Isaacs' character-led films, self-presentation is action. Over Jamie's shoulder, Laura-Anne holds her counsel: at least he's here with her now, unlike the inconstant Ben, busy growing into a "true Siddick man" of the sea, a budding fisherman with his eye on the prospects beyond the shore.

"There's plenty of fish in the sea – that's what her daddy taught. Which is all very well if you wanted to go out with a fish, she thought."

Will Laura-Anne, too, have to cast her net wider? The wind blows, the turbines turn, the seasons roll round. The sun once more hangs long and low on the water.

Isaacs doesn't try to pin voiceover words on the seven-wived Philip. For one thing, according to his sister, who (Isaacs aside) provides the one and only intrusion of the lay world into his domestic kingdom, Philip has always been "more of a leader than a follower"; even when he was but a young Jewish DJ, she recalls, he had frequent overnight 'followers' she'd find herself making morning tea for. For another thing, Philip doesn't need any further platform for his voice than the camera already gives him. We first meet him in the field, barking orders at horses and wives alike: "If you don't handle them right they do get a bit wild."

Most astounding are the family dinners he convenes to gather his women in guitar-accompanied hymns before picking up a microphone and haranguing them at length, one and all, for their moral and spiritual failures. "Everything's about yielding, and I can feel that you're not yielding," he bemoans, persisting with his conflation of horses and women. "I cannot take you with me around this bend. We're not talking about something you can blag here." By universal standards the man is a tyrant and bully, but it's not clear that he's also a hypocrite, and early on Isaacs deftly steers us beyond smug mockery with the observation that Philip clearly isn't interested in equality between the sexes.

Isaacs states: *Philip may be certain of the road to Godliness, but he hadn't mastered the secondhand furniture business.* Certainly none of it looks easy, and Isaacs identifies *a real loneliness in Phil still*, but this is a man with a vision, a mission from God, and aggro aside there's little in the way of vulnerability he's prepared to show us. On the other hand, as with Laura-Anne and her boys, there are seven other characters in this set-up. Why had they rejected contemporary wisdom, wonders Isaacs? Had they found in the Old Testament the way to live?

It's not clear that the film passes 'The Bechdel Test' (cartoonist Alison Bechdel's semi-satirical standard for judging whether a film has female characters who get to talk about something other than a man) – but as Isaacs endeavours to individualise each of the wives, several of them own their motives, confusion and pain. Judith, his first wife and the only Jew of the seven, straightforwardly admits to missing the time she used to get with Philip and the sense that she wasn't alone. Tracy starts the film cast out of the house for her apostate ways, and is one of two wives who recognise no claim to their own children if they had to leave the household ("Phil will only decide based on what God says"). She also seems quite content to accept Philip's characterisation of her as a disruptive and pagan influence.

Most vivid is the case of Chava, a wallflower who Philip later moves out of the house like a piece of furniture, and berates for letting herself go. When she admits Isaacs into her confidence, her open tears are disarming: Philip is the first person to really know her, she says, the good, the bad and the ugly, no matter a long, unconsummated precious marriage. She shows us a painting of a dancing lady in red, flanked by a peripheral, supplicant old maid, and explains how God wants her to be the lady centre-frame, dancing with her true love. She doesn't want to be returned to God like an unopened letter; she wants to be opened up. It's a scene of quiet, desperate sadness nestled inside a quizzical comedy of human perversity.

Nick Bradshaw is *Sight & Sound*'s Web Editor and a film critic of 20 years' standing, having begun his career working for the film section at *Time Out* and also been published by the *Guardian*, *Independent*, *Times*, *Telegraph* and *LA Weekly*. He has a BA in Politics, Philosophy and Economics and a MFA in Film/ Video from CalArts

Are Racists and Bankers Not Human Also?
The quality of mercy in the films of Marc Isaacs
by Noel Megahey

'The quality of mercy is not strain'd.
It droppeth as the gentle rain from heaven
Upon the place beneath. It is twice blest.
It blesseth him that gives, and him that takes.'

William Shakespeare, *The Merchant of Venice*, Act 4 Scene 1

While remaining true to the essential themes that are consistent throughout all of his work, *All White in Barking* and *Men of the City* at the same time demonstrate the distinct evolution of style and approach that has taken place since the earlier documentary work of Marc Isaacs. The distance is most pronounced if we look back as far as Isaacs' first short film, *Lift* (2001), filmed almost entirely within the confines of a lift in a Margate tower block. Regularly taking up position in a corner of the lift over a period of two months, sharing a small space with the inhabitants of the tower block, gradually getting them to open up small but revealing aspects of their lives, it was the inspired choice of this little common in-between space, between home and the outside world, that Isaacs unexpectedly found a perfect little microcosm of a section of

British society that had previously never had a voice, or indeed anyone willing or interested enough to lend a sympathetic ear to their stories.

It's the stories of little people, unacknowledged by a world that is not so much uncaring as largely unaware of their existence, that would also become the subject of Marc Isaacs' subsequent two documentaries, *Travellers* (2002) and *Calais: The Last Border* (2003). Finding another two regular, everyday, neutral and intermediate places of interconnection – train stations and a port – Isaacs was able to tap into an even greater cross-section of modern society and reveal how the ordinary can become extraordinary when it comes to people's emotions, feelings and experiences; their suffering, their hopes and their fears. The evolution between the first three films of Marc Isaacs is small but clearly perceptible, each respective film being a little more ambitious, externally widening its scope while at the same time delving deeper internally into those qualities that, for better or worse, make us all human.

From a small space of some 40 square feet in *Lift*, *Travellers* extends its view to consider the often ordinary impulses and reasons that drive people even a short distance from one part of the country to another for reasons that we, probably caught up in our own concerns and having never spoken to strangers on a train in the way Isaacs does, would never have imagined. *Calais: The Last Border* expands this viewpoint even further, showing how people attempt to better their lives and start anew through emigration, the film taking into consideration not only the more obvious question of the much maligned figure of the illegal immigrant – referred to pejoratively as Asylum Seekers by disdainful Calais booze-cruisers in the film – but also looking at the reasons why British people leave the UK. In each film, Marc Isaacs manages to shed a light on a hitherto little explored aspect of British society, putting a human story behind headlines and statistics, giving the vaguely threatening stranger next to you a rather more sympathetic human face.

All White in Barking (2008) and *Men of the City* (2009) continue this view of looking beneath the surface of ordinary people's lives and giving a voice to the common man, while at the same time extending it to take into consideration two subjects even more challenging than the humanising of the asylum seeker. Between them, the films look at two other figures in contemporary society whom it is far too convenient to make easy assumptions about and dismiss under lurid headlines calculated to inspire shock and outrage in the public. But are racists and bankers not human also? Are they not capable of feelings like the rest of us? If we prick them, do they not bleed? The reference to Shakespeare's *The Merchant of Venice* is doubly appropriate in this case, as between them *All White in Barking* and *Men of the City* deal with questions of prejudice, fear and suspicion in relation to racial differences as well as towards banking institutions; but in the case of Marc Isaacs at least, the quality of mercy is not strained.

The fact that racists are people too should be self-evident, but at the start of *All White in Barking* at least, the more liberal, cosmopolitan viewer's indulgence is tested to its limit. The nature of the casual and in some cases wilful bigotry of a few examples of the sizeable number of the population of Barking and Dagenham, many of whom voted for the openly racist British National Party, the BNP, at the last elections, is a shocking reminder of the blind intolerance, prejudice and ignorance that exists in some parts of the country. If these people can't be bothered to examine their own consciences, see the contradictions, untruths and ignorance that underpin these beliefs and question their abhorrent and socially unacceptable views, why indeed should the viewer have any time for them? Clearly, no amount of intelligent persuasion is going to make them change their minds.

It's a testament to the qualities of Marc Isaacs' skill as an interviewer and as a filmmaker that he is not only able to elicit such frank views from ordinary people confronted by a man with a camera following them around asking these awkward questions without raising their ire, but that he isn't prepared to make such quick and easy judgments. Going out of his way to introduce neighbours of different races who ordinarily wouldn't give each other the time of day, Isaacs does in fact find a means to challenge those views and even change them. It might seem like a questionable practice for a documentary filmmaker to impose his will upon a subject in this way, rather than adhering to the more conventional fly-on-the-wall non-interventionist approach, but this is part of Marc Isaacs' singular talent, and it's one that is justified by the even greater results and insights that it yields.

Rather than adopt a distanced approach, employing psychologists, social anthropologists, experts or politicians to comment dispassionately and no doubt disapprovingly on the phenomenon, Isaacs is much more interested in the voice of the people. And more than just being interested in what people have to say – as he has demonstrated abundantly in his earlier films – Marc Isaacs is also interested in people themselves. He cares not only about what they think, he wants to understand why they think what they think and he even wants to help them. Isaacs doesn't introduce a white couple to their African neighbours just to patronise them or show them the error of their ways, but rather he shows that attitudes can be changed if one is willing to listen to those who feel threatened or disenfranchised and engage with their concerns. And who knows – maybe one day "Freddie the Albanian" next door will just be called "Freddie".

That's an admirable aim and Isaacs makes the point most persuasively, but it's the least of his achievements in *All White in Barking*. Despite the right-minded viewer's instinctive revulsion for the blatant intolerance and unthinking prejudice in the people they initially encounter, it becomes clear that many are actually decent people with genuine concerns who mean no real harm to anyone. They just feel threatened and isolated by the huge changes they see happening in the community they have lived in all their lives through a sudden influx of foreigners whose traditions, culture, religion, language and sense of dress they do not understand, while they themselves belong to an older generation that is not of the nature to accept change or differences willingly.

Remarkably, Marc Isaacs captures this not only through his interviewees but, in not so many words, through the faces from a bygone age who stare uncomprehendingly as the shutters come down on a local butcher's shop, forced to close down after 40 years, their wares no longer catering to the more exotic tastes of the town's changing population. Much too easy to dismiss, they too are people nonetheless, people whose voice needs to be heard and understood. If the expression of those views is misguided and exploited by those with more sinister objectives, Isaacs shows that their concerns are nonetheless genuine, and politicians, journalists or anyone else inclined to dismiss their views as those of an ignorant and uneducated mob do so at their peril.

It's a sign of our times that it's not only the asylum seeker, the economic migrant and the racist who are all too casually demonised, but the aforementioned politicians and even journalists have recently come in for their share of invective from a public seeking accountability for the state of the country. At present, however, there doesn't seem to be any sector of society that has generated more headlines and hatred, yet whose role and function in the meltdown of the economy is least understood, than that of the banking institutions. In his following of several financial brokers in London's financial district, commonly known as the City, Isaacs confronts perhaps his most challenging subject, the one surprisingly most resistant to revealing any semblance of humanity lying underneath. If Isaacs' approach is rather more abstract and open in *Men of the City*, it's appropriate when the conclusions are much less clear.

Typically, Marc Isaacs approaches the subject from an unexpected but fascinating angle, considering City workers from a number of varied and contrasting viewpoints. There are other people who work in the City, and one can even catch a glimpse of the homeless on its streets, but in addition to the more obvious financial brokers, Isaacs' film takes into consideration the attempts of a humble road sweeper and a sandwich-board man who are also working there and attempting to make something of their lives. On the part of any other filmmaker, the choice of such contrasting figures within the City would seem to be a deliberate and obvious editorial decision to throw the greed of the financial institutions into sharp relief, but with Marc Isaacs one feels that the approach is more egalitarian, the study more humanitarian, the conclusions not already prejudged.

'Will you sweep away the righteous with the wicked, what if there are righteous men in the city?' (Genesis)

With its portentous Old Testament biblical quote from Genesis relating to Abraham's plea for the sparing of Sodom and Gomorrah, it's evident from the outset that the quality of mercy in Marc Isaacs' previous films is going to be most tested in the environment of the City, the search for those elusive human qualities more difficult to find, and the filmmaker accordingly casts his net wider and without preconceptions. Rather than using the obvious contrast between the common man working on the streets and the educated rich man bartering in the bull-ring of the stock market to make his point, what emerges from *Men of the City* is a Darwinian struggle for the survival of the fittest on all levels of society. Mercy is no more readily shown towards failure in the financial sector than it is towards the man who leaves his post as a sign-holder to look after his sick daughter in hospital. Their lives filled with the unending struggle to simply survive, to continually keep one step ahead of imminent disaster, can they still retain their dignity and humanity in the process?

It's clear that Marc Isaacs wants to believe it can still be found and he probes his subjects even as they are rebuffed in their search for employment, see their large profits dwindle and slip from their grasp as the market reels from the collapse of a major American bank, and as they consider the prospect of finding themselves on the scrapheap. Norman, about to be downsized after 32 years from Master of the Universe to Master of his own Destiny, when asked by Isaacs if he might not have wanted to have children at some stage and maybe have lived his life differently, has no regrets. Or to be more accurate, he has had no time for regrets or even time to think that there might be any other way of living – but he is now willing to consider other possibilities. Similarly, the filmmaker is rewarded with a rare smile that appears on the face of one financial worker, David, as he photographs his children – a sign that he still has a grasp of the things that are important. But his hobby and his children still remain marginal, a weekend diversion that has to be suppressed at the start of the working week, his attention consumed by the anticipation and fear of what the markets might hold in store.

The apocalyptic nature of the constant downpour of rain, the edges of humanity blurred through rain-streaked windows, Michel Duvoisin's score taken to more expressive levels in its menacing tones, all indicate that the filmmaker is in despair of finding any human decency in his subjects this time around and is indeed prepared to let them all be swept away in a biblical Day of Judgement. This is no 'gentle rain from heaven'. But what if there is one righteous man in the City? In one moment that recalls the filmmaker's style of old, Isaacs speaks to a random worker contemplating the Thames in his lunch break, who shares the story of a woman he once rescued from the river. It's a small act of mercy that makes no headlines, goes unrewarded and would never be known were it not for Marc Isaacs' camera. Would each of the subjects of *Men of the City* not have done the same in this man's place? If there is one righteous man in the City, might there not be fifty with the capacity to also demonstrate their human qualities, given the opportunity?

The question is left open for the viewer to consider, and the answer is by no means clear or certain, but without evidence to the contrary, Marc Isaacs seems to spare the men of the City from the wrath of an Old Testament God, the rain clearing to reveal a rainbow forming over the business district. It's an extraordinary effect that risks appearing calculated, sentimental and manipulative; a hopelessly naïve belief in the underlying goodness of mankind that it would seem hasn't been adequately proved. On the other hand, witnessed by Steve, the sweeper overlooking his patch of the City, there's a sense that the financial meltdown has indeed been a kind of biblical deluge that has tested each of the subjects of *Men of the City* and the director's faith in their underlying humanity. What emerges here, as it does in Marc Isaacs' other films, is people's extraordinary capacity for resilience in the face of adversity, a resilience buoyed by a spark of humanity that is perhaps more deeply submerged, but not yet completely extinguished.

Noel Megahey writes for the on-line film site *The Digital Fix*.

Out of Screen, *Out of Time*: The Temporality of Exhibited Cinema by Laura Rascaroli

The relocation of the experience of the cinema to the art gallery and the museum has liberated filmic time. No longer constrained by the strict stipulations of theatrical screenings (rarely infringed historically, and mostly by major art film directors of the likes of Stanley Kubrick, Andrei Tarkovsky and Luchino Visconti), nor by the requirements of narrative development, with its chronological chains of events and its cause-and-effect patterns, film finds itself rethinking and reinventing time as its spectator knows it: the time of production, the time of the text, and the time of consumption, first of all; and then everyday time, human time, remembered time, the time of the event, cinematic time.

The title of Marc Isaacs's installation, *Out of Time*, acknowledges the momentousness of the filmmaker's gesture of taking his films into another temporal dimension — the one that is proffered by the context of the art institution. In fact, the title is semantically ambiguous and could equally refer to the act of taking filmic images out of their narrative chronology and refashioning them according to a different temporality; or to the viewer's experience of filmed images not in their original temporal contexts but rather the here and now in which they come to fruition; or, again, to the emptying out and annulment of time, as produced by the forms of fragmentation, of looping and of repetition that come about in the art gallery more freely than in the linear filmic medium. What's more, if we draw on the artist's notes accompanying the installation, the title could even refer to finding oneself outside the capitalist time of production. For as Isaacs writes, 'The idea of *Out of Time* emerged during a period of frustration whilst waiting on funding for a feature film. These periods of waiting always provoke reflection, as well as imaginings of future works.' The interruption of productive time, thus, causes a state of mind that can engender frustration, but also free time, fuelling creative possibilities — including those of imagining a different (filmic) temporality, not dependent on the all too restrictive standards of the film and TV industry.

Expectation and waiting, suspension and temporal emptiness are recurrent features of the four pieces of *Out of Time*. *Moments of Silence* splices together a series of introspective shots from Marc Isaacs's significant body of non-fiction work, in which the characters, mostly feeling overwhelmed by difficult thoughts, pause and fall silent, seemingly dwelling on their past, contemplating their current ordeals, or worrying about the future. In *Notes on Bangladesh*, on the other hand, the filmed subjects anxiously wait for the heavy monsoon rains and the catastrophic flooding that periodically submerges their villages. In *Sisters*, two ageing siblings sit next to each other in a pub, waiting for instructions from the filmmaker, which never come, whilst watching the time go by. Finally, *Rainy Days* remobilises some of the same images of suspension and waiting from these three works, splicing them together in a sort of alternate montage and to a new soundtrack. Individually and together, these installations insert the spectator into hiatuses and gaps, where the time of action is suspended, and story with it.

The temporal structure of these works, indeed, is anti-narrative. *Moments of Silence* takes the form of a collection, a compilation; the shots are taken out of their contexts, and a spectator unfamiliar with Isaacs's films will have no reference-points to situate them in a prior narrative continuum. The temporality of a compilation of fragments drawn from pre-existing works is disjointed, allusive. This temporality clearly gestures towards a missing whole, but also isolates single moments, now spliced together according to a different logic — one governed not by cause and effect, but by similarity, contrast, or ineffable affinities, and which shift again at each new sequential configuration. The looping form of *Moments of Silence* generates repetitiousness; however, even the act itself of repeating creates a difference, as Gilles Deleuze (1994) has shown us. Taking these images out of their narrative chronology and reusing them in looping chains produces indeed an altogether new temporality of suspension.

Notes on Bangladesh, meanwhile, is a notebook film — a set of notes taken by means of the camera rather than the pen, a highly personal and — usually — private form of filmmaking and videomaking in the main, used to make a record of possible settings and characters in view of a future film. In this sense, and also on account of its setting, *Notes on Bangladesh* can be said to be mindful of works such as *Sopralluoghi in Palestina per il Vangelo Secondo Matteo* (*Location Hunting in Palestine*, 1965), *Appunti per un film sull'India* (*Notes Towards a Film on India*, 1968), and *Appunti per un'Orestiade africana* (*Notes Towards an African Orestes*, 1970) by Pier Paolo Pasolini, a filmmaker who frequently used the notebook form. While Pasolini talked over the images, however, Isaacs lets his subjects speak directly to the camera or simply fall silent, refraining from interpretation. In these ways, *Notes on Bangladesh* maintains the modest structure of the notebook, which is receptive to the mundane, fragmentary, is ongoing and open, and does not attempt a strong narrative organisation of its materials. It presents us with a temporality that is raw.

Of the four pieces, *Sisters* is the most traditionally filmic and the most palpably narrative, though its story is minimalistic, focusing on two aging women who simply sit side by side in a pub, perhaps waiting for instructions on the part of the director — and thus waiting (in vain) for the eventful time of the cinema to begin. Their understated gestures and the way they sit in relation to each other are revealing of habit and familiarity, thus suggesting a temporality of everydayness, repetition and recurrence. On the other hand, the film builds up tension and anticipation, exacerbated by the weight of waiting, by the lack of action and the temporal emptiness. *Sisters* is a piece that materialises the feeling of time through its slow unfolding. Indeed, slowness is also a mark of the other two works, which invite us to stay with the characters at their times of inaction and introspection, and to take in landscapes patiently.

Finally, *Rainy Days* radicalises the experiment of *Moments of Silence* by combining shots of the three-different works, further isolating them from their narrative contexts — for any naturalistic sound is replaced by Matej Dimlic's allusive musical composition of the same title, suggestive of subjectivity and dream. *Rainy Days* is inspired by the concept of the triptych, an art-historical form conjoining three panels with distinct images, which thus enter into a reciprocal relationship that the spectators are invited to explore and to imagine. In spite of combining the images, however, the triptych ultimately emphasises their incommensurability, the split and the gap separating them. As Gilles Deleuze (2003) has written, in the triptych 'An immense space-time unites all things, *but only by introducing between them the distances of a Sahara, the centuries of an aeon'* (60) (emphasis in the original). Carlos Vara Sánchez has commented that 'This difference of temporospatial potential is inherent to triptychs and implies a feeling of irresolution in what we are contemplating. A triptych breathes in a specific way, its space is open to interpretations, to wandering, and its architecture generates forces which traverse the three different panels.' (40). The temporality of *Rainy Days* is, on this account, paradoxical, suggesting all at once the universality of the human experience and the discontinuities that haunt it.

Together with *Moments of Silence*, *Rainy Days* is an example of what Philippe Dubois (2016), working within his category of *cinéma exposé* (exhibited cinema), terms the de-/re-composed film. The work of the filmmaker here is a re-editing of fragments, which, starting from the de-composition and dismemberment of the original film, yields a reconfiguration that is a new work. As Dubois has observed, de-/re-composing a film is a labour of research, of scrutiny, of investigation. *Moments of Silence* and *Rainy Days* constitute a filmmaker's search into his own work; in particular, they are a study of images of human faces and gestures that become isolated within the works' discontinuous fabric. Also in narrative cinema, close-ups are for the spectator moments of pure contemplation, when the time of the story halts and a different time — or an out-of-time — imposes itself. In these moments, there is no action, no development, no new information, no progression; there is only pregnant suspension. The close-up invites us to intimately connect with the character pictured onscreen and scrutinise his/her emotions, exploring the face as a human landscape, revealing the subject's innermost feelings. In both *Moments of Silence* and *Rainy Days*, the suspension expands to occupy the entire text. It is a modality of viewing that creates a more profound intimacy, further heightened by the sorrow, melancholy and grief experienced by the characters — who, moreover, are not fictional personae but actual people facing real ordeals. These installations make us experience intimacy in public. For Giuliana Bruno (2016), indeed, both cinema and the museum activate a 'layered form of projection that activates public intimacy on the surface of things.' (36).

The re-composition of isolated moments according to an inner logic of allusions and connections in *Moments of Silence*, the juxtaposition of diverse images shot in different places and at different times ('the distances of a Sahara, the centuries of an aeon') of *Rainy Days*, the sophisticated if minimalistic filmic montage of *Sisters*, and the paratactic assemblage of impressions of *Notes on Bangladesh* — such are the diverse signifying strategies mobilised by each of the four installations. And yet, montage in *Out of Time* is not just internal to the four separate works. *Rainy Days*, in fact, promotes a relational reading of the other three installations by bringing them together, thus encouraging the spectator to a work of mental montage. By moving through the space of the gallery and between the four screens, indeed, the spectator not only experiences each work in its own right but is also invited to compare and connect them, thus operating a personal de-/re-composition. The function of montage comes to be opened up to the spectator, who actualises it via a to-and-fro movement that is mental and physical, shifting from screen to screen, from image to image.

This sort of proprioceptive montage, which relies on the movement of bodies, of gazes within and across the gallery, and on the sensations that this movement elicits, has also the effect of spatializing time: we situate the four works in relation to each other as we negotiate the space between the screens — a distance that is at once spatial and temporal, for it concretises the simultaneity, distance, parallelism, and difference that unite or separate the images. It is in this projective space, at once physical and mental, that the four installations enter into a profound reciprocal relationship — one which is thus located 'out of screen', as well as 'out of time'.

Works cited

Bruno, Giuliana, 'Cinema, Museum, and the Art of Projection', *Extended Temporalities: Transient Visions in the Museum and in Art*, edited by Alessandro Bordina, Vincenzo Estremo, and Francesco Federici, 17–39, Mimesis International, 2016.

Deleuze, Gilles, *Difference and Repetition*, translated by Paul Patton, Columbia University Press, 1994.

Deleuze, Gilles, *Francis Bacon: The Logic of Sensation*, translated by Daniel W. Smith, University of Minnesota Press, 2003.

Dubois, Philippe, 'Le cinéma exposé: Essai de catégorisation', *Extended Temporalities: Transient Visions in the Museum and in Art*, edited by Alessandro Bordina, Vincenzo Estremo, and Francesco Federici, 41–71, Mimesis International, 2016.

Sánchez, Carlos Vara, 'Bill Viola's *Nantes Triptych*: Unearthing the Sources of its Condensed Temporality', *Aniki: Revista Portuguesa da Imagem em Movimento* 2 (1): 35–48, 2014.

Laura Rascaroli is Professor of Film and Screen Media at University College Cork, Ireland. She is the author and editor of several volumes, including *The Personal Camera: Subjective Cinema and the Essay Film* (2009), *Crossing New Europe: Postmodern Travel and the European Road Movie* (2006), co-written with Ewa Mazierska, and *Antonioni: Centenary Essays* (2011), co-edited with John David Rhodes. Her new book, *How the Essay Film Thinks*, was published by Oxford University Press in 2017. She is general editor of *Alphaville: Journal of Film and Screen Media*.

Film Information

Lift (2001)

Filmed and directed by Marc Isaacs
Editor - Russell Crockett
Language: English; Sound: Original stereo;
Colour
Original aspect ratio: 1.33 full frame
Length: 24:27 minutes

Travellers (2002)

Filmed and directed by Marc Isaacs
Editor - David Charap
Language: English; Sound: Original stereo;
Colour
Original aspect ratio: 1.33 full frame
Length: 47:46 minutes

Calais: The Last Border (2003)

Filmed and directed by Marc Isaacs
Editor - David Charap
Language: English; Sound: Original stereo;
Colour
Original aspect ratio: 1.33 full frame
Length: 58:53 minutes

Someday My Prince Will Come (2005)

Filmed and directed by Marc Isaacs
Written by Jonathan Ruffle
Editor – David Charap
Language: English; Sound: Original stereo;
Colour;
Original aspect ratio: 1.33 full frame
Length: 49:19 minutes

Philip and His Seven Wives (2006)

Filmed and directed by Marc Isaacs
Editor – Ollie Huddleston
Language: English; Sound: Original stereo;
Colour;
Original aspect ratio: 1.33 full frame
Length: 69:27 minutes

All White in Barking (2008)

Filmed and directed by Marc Isaacs
Editor - David Charap
Language: English; Sound: Original stereo;
Colour
Original aspect ratio: 1.78:1
Length: 72:26 minutes

Men of the City (2009)

Filmed and directed by Marc Isaacs
Editor - David Charap
Language: English; Sound: Original stereo;
Colour
Original aspect ratio: 1.78:1
Length: 58:14 minutes

The Old Man and His Bed (2011)

Filmed and directed by Marc Isaacs
Editor – Burt Hunger
Language: English; Sound: Original stereo;
Colour
Original aspect ratio: 1.78:1
Length: 7:20 minutes

Outside the Court (2011)

Filmed and directed by Marc Isaacs
Editor – Burt Hunger
Language: English; Sound: Original stereo;
Colour
Original aspect ratio: 1.78:1
Length: 58:45 minutes

The Road – A Story of Life and Death (2013)

Filmed and directed by Marc Isaacs
Editor – David Charap
Language: English; Sound: Original stereo;
Colour
Original aspect ratio: 1.78:1
Length: 75:12 minutes

Outsiders (2014)

Filmed and directed by Marc Isaacs
Editor - Aldo Paternostro
Language: English; Sound: Original stereo;
Colour
Original aspect ratio: 1.78:1
Length: 18:00 minutes

Touched by Murder (2016)

Filmed and directed by Marc Isaacs
Editor – Aldo Paternostro
Language: English; Sound: Original stereo;
Colour
Original aspect ratio: 1.78:1
Length: 16:30 minutes

When Night Falls (2016)

Filmed and directed by Marc Isaacs
Editor – Estephan Wagner
Language: English; Sound: Original stereo;
Colour
Original aspect ratio: 1.78:1
Length: 18:44 minutes

Sisters (2017)

Filmed and directed by Marc Isaacs
Editor Dave Briggs
Language: English; Sound: Original stereo;
Colour
Original aspect ratio: 1.33 full frame
Length: 7:35 minutes

Notes on Bangladesh (2017)

Filmed and directed by Marc Isaacs
Editor – Dave Briggs
Language: English; Sound: Original stereo;
Colour
Original aspect ratio: 1.78:1
Length: 23:41 minutes

Rainy Days (2017)

Filmed and directed by Marc Isaacs and Matej Dimlic
Editor – Matej Dimlic
Language: Bengali (English sub-titles) Sound: Original stereo;
Colour
Original aspect ratio: 1.78:1
Length: 6:00 minutes

Moments of Silence (2017)

Filmed and directed by Marc Isaacs
Editor – Marc Isaacs
Language: English; Sound: Original stereo;
Colour
Original aspect ratio: 1.78:1
Length: 5:00 minutes (loop)